THIS BOOK BELONGS TO:

____

____

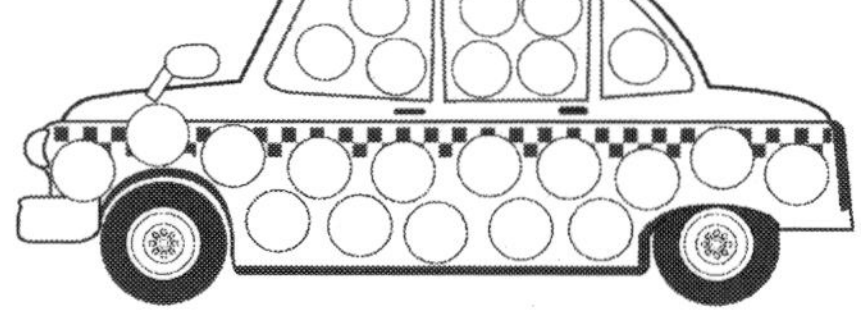

5

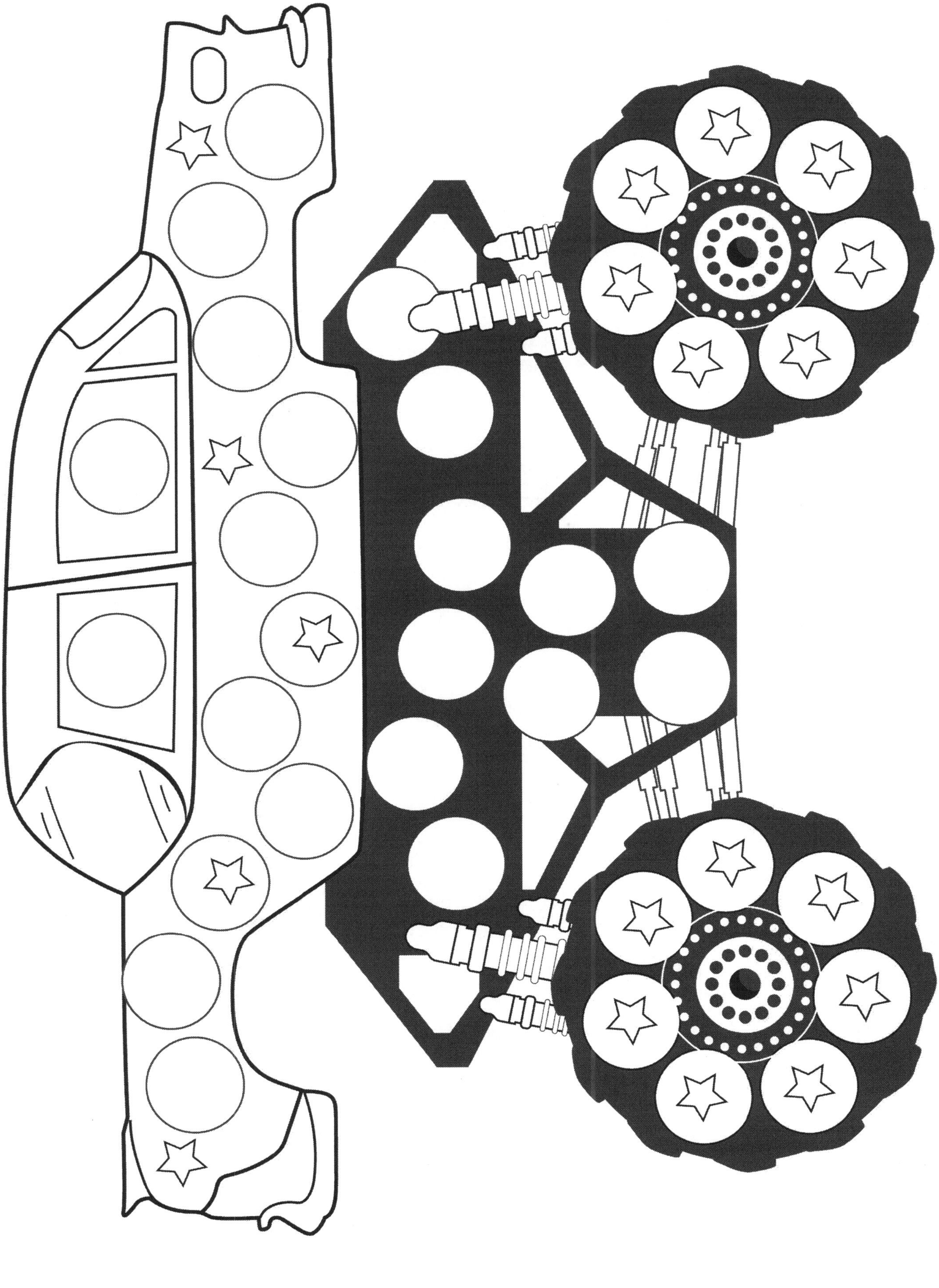

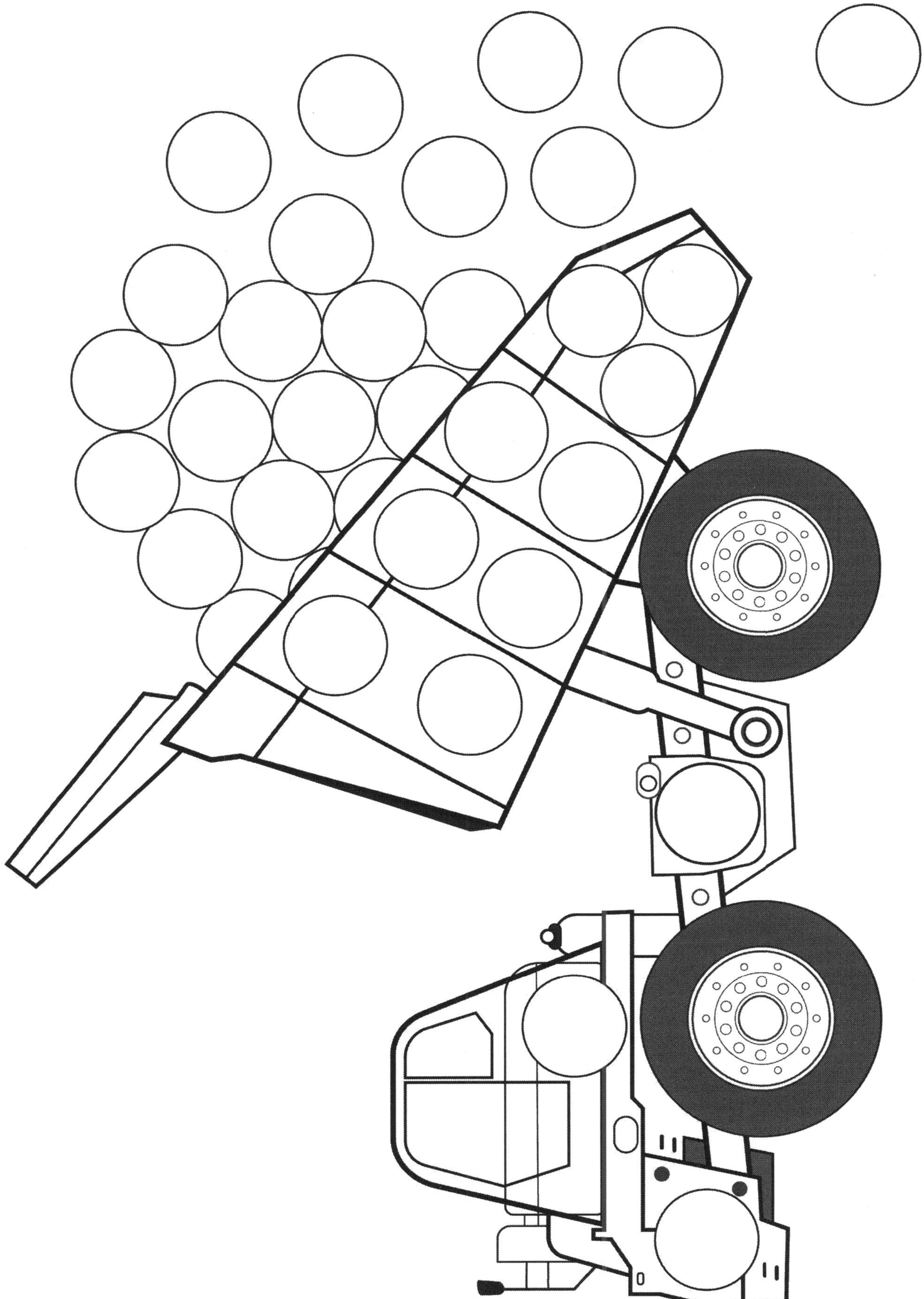

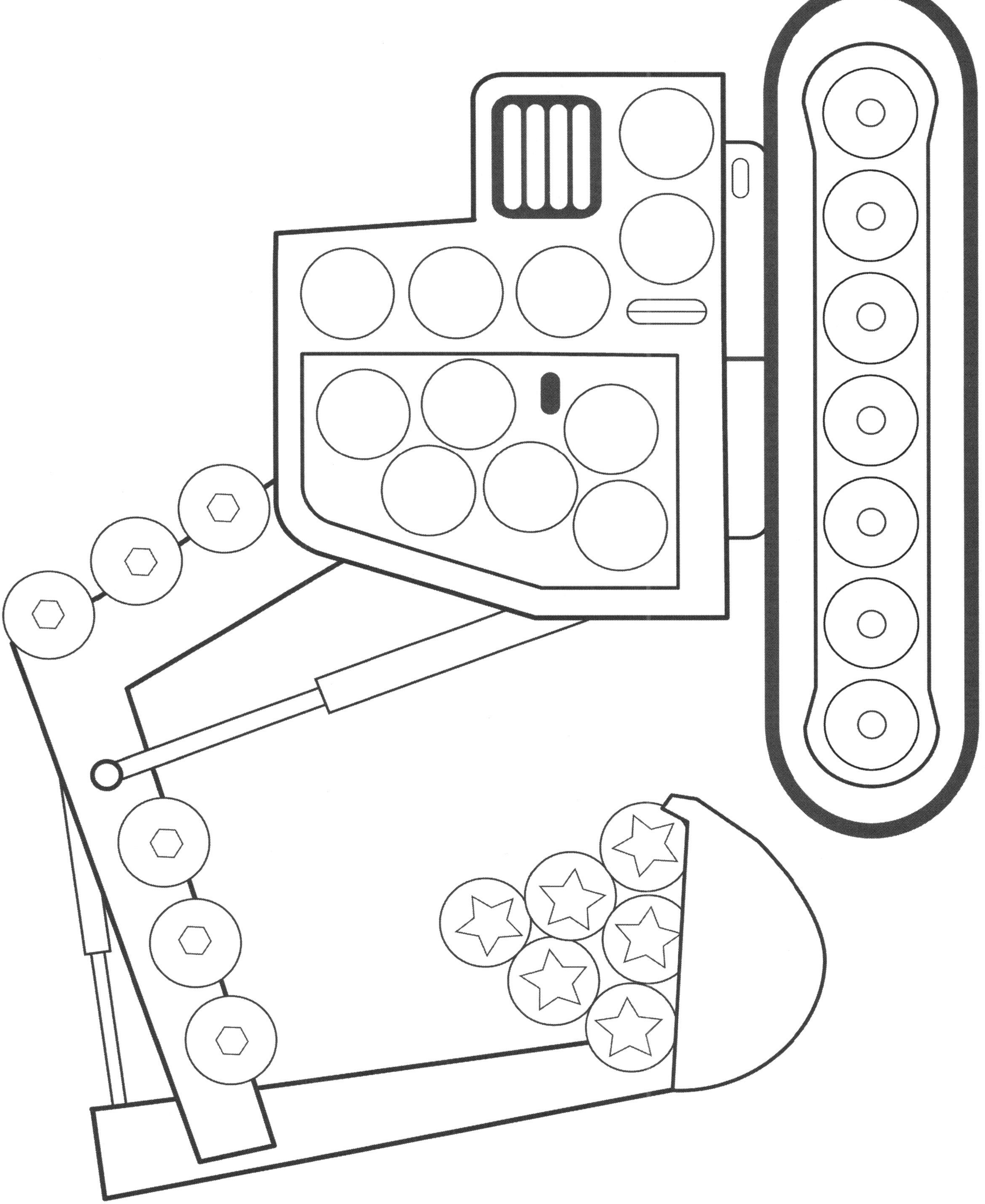

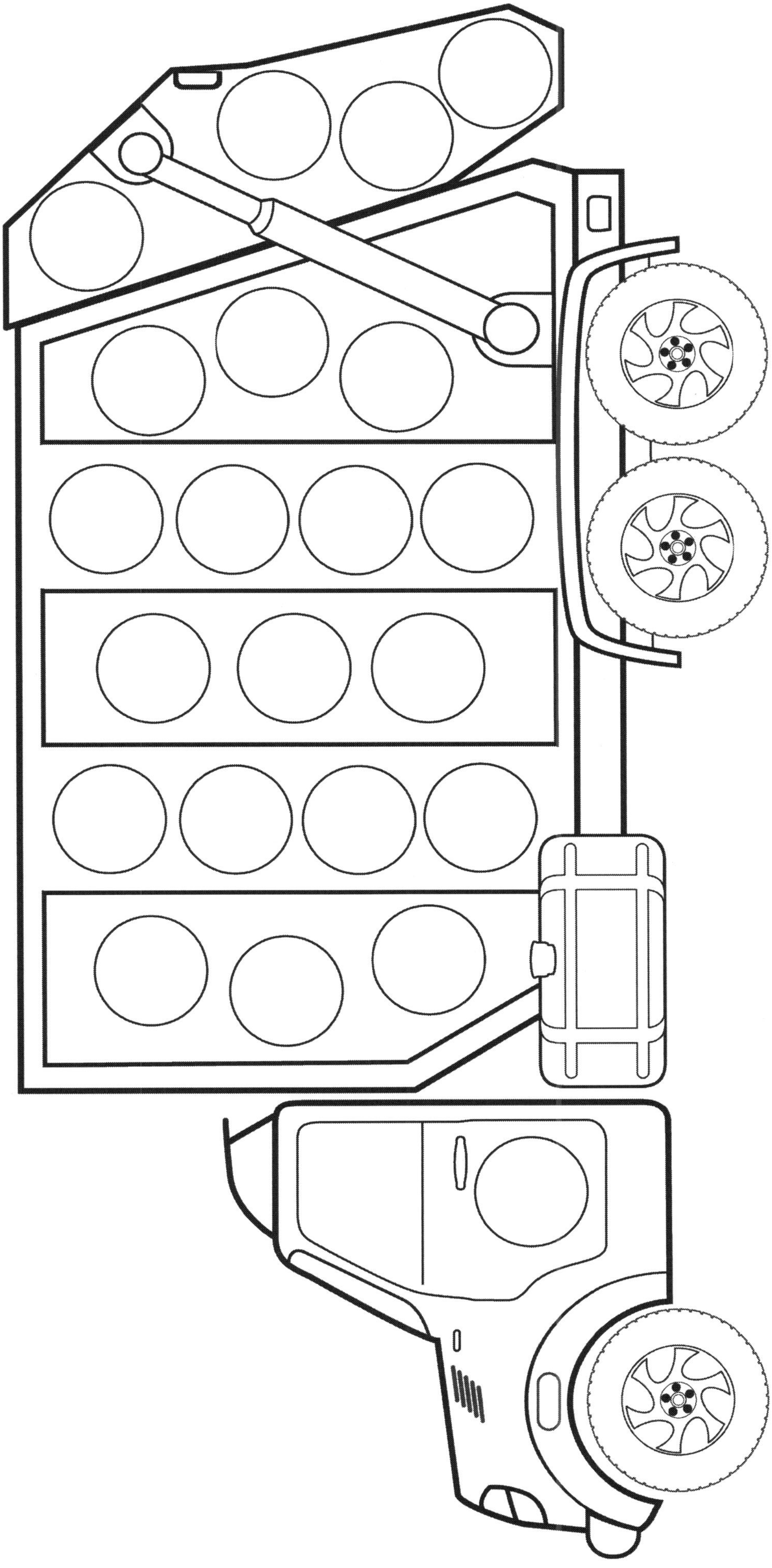

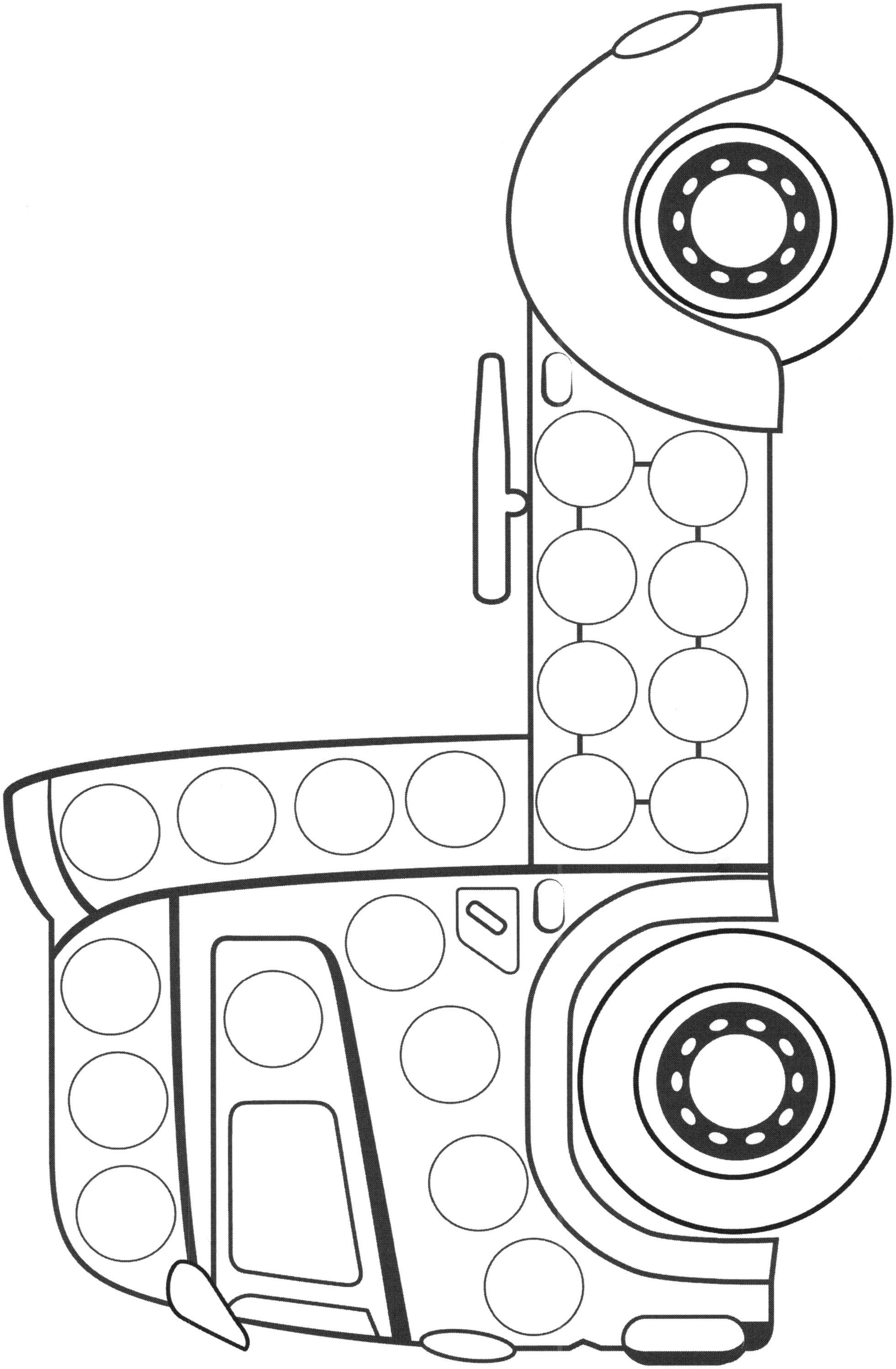

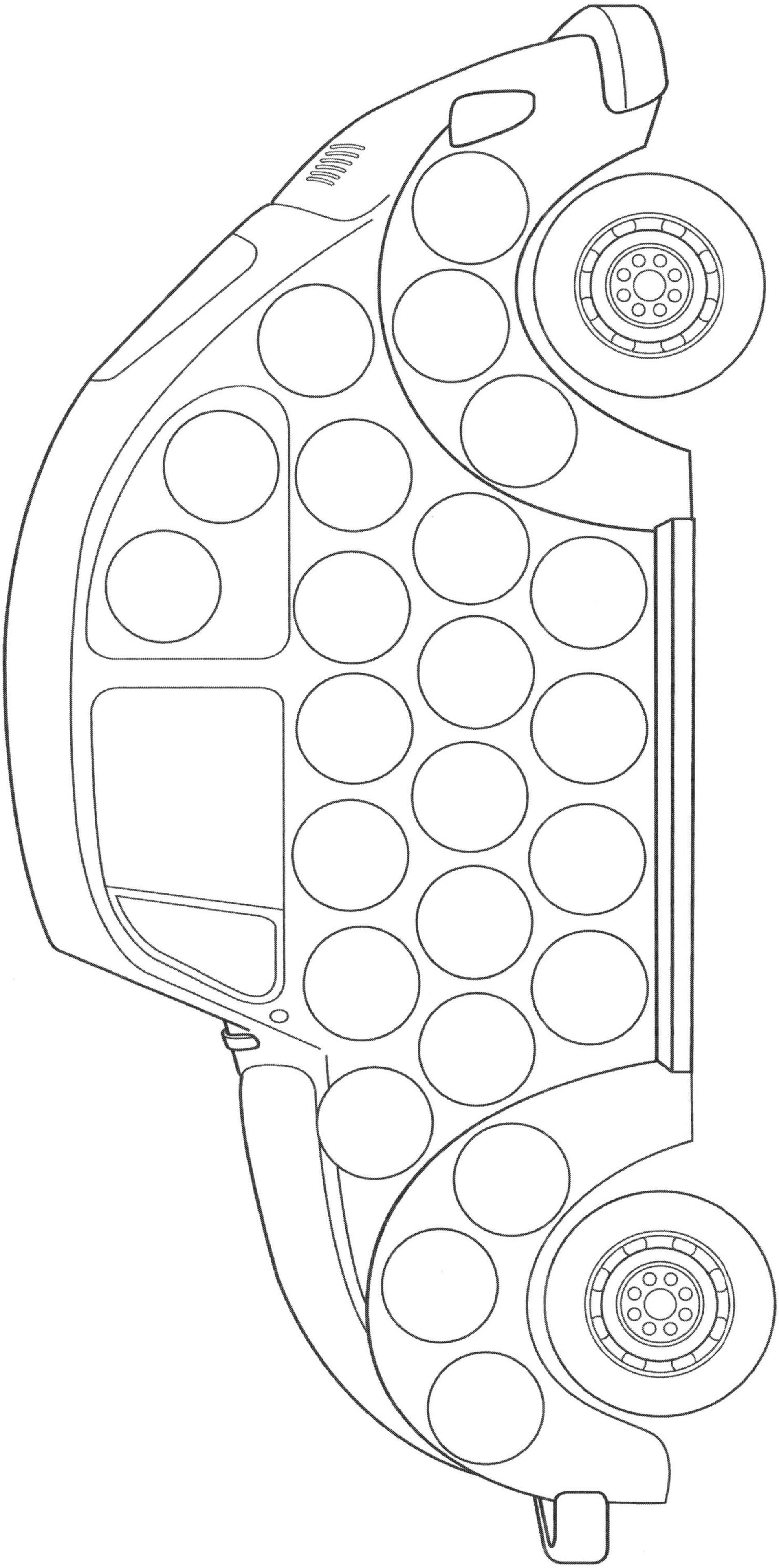

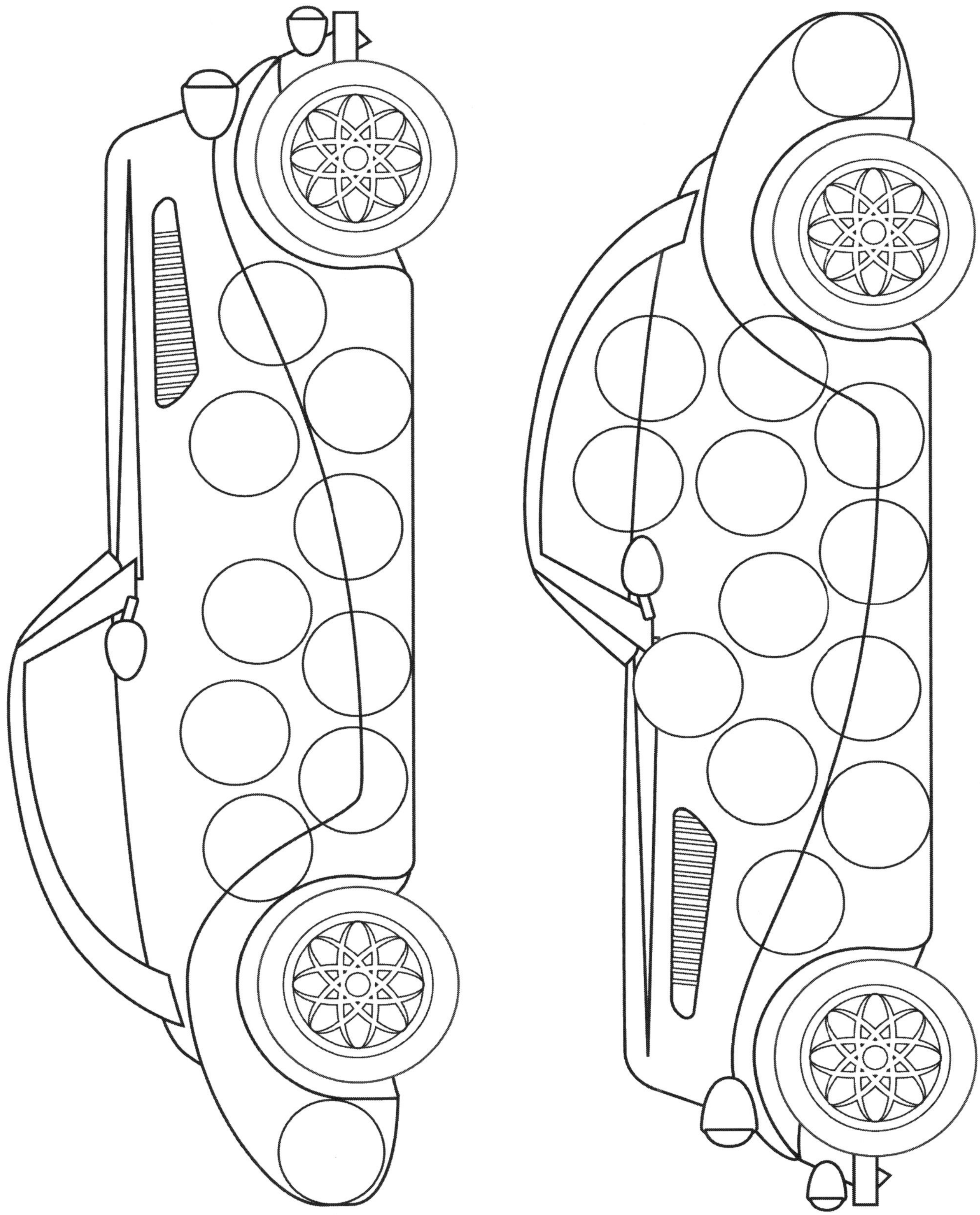

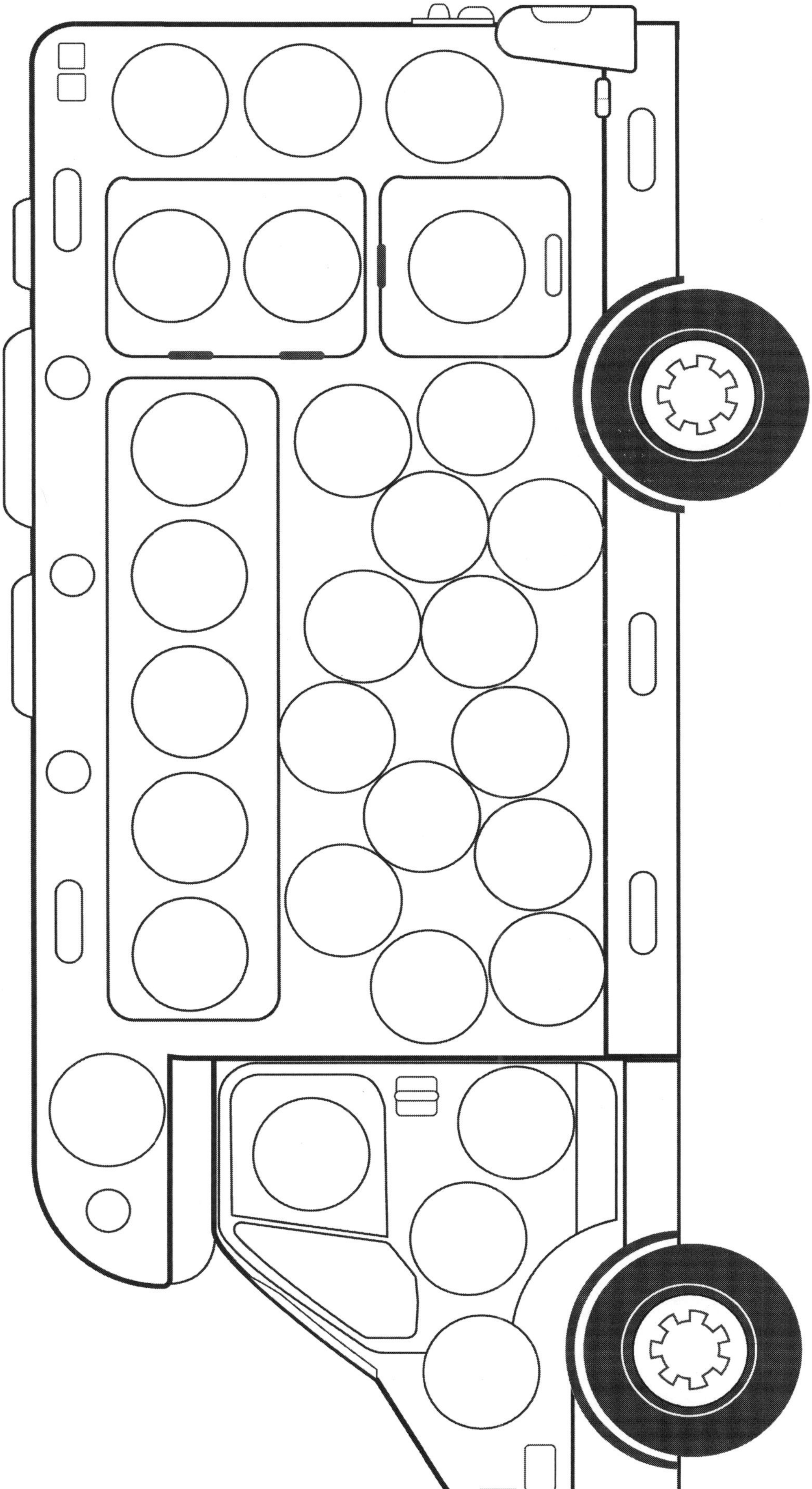

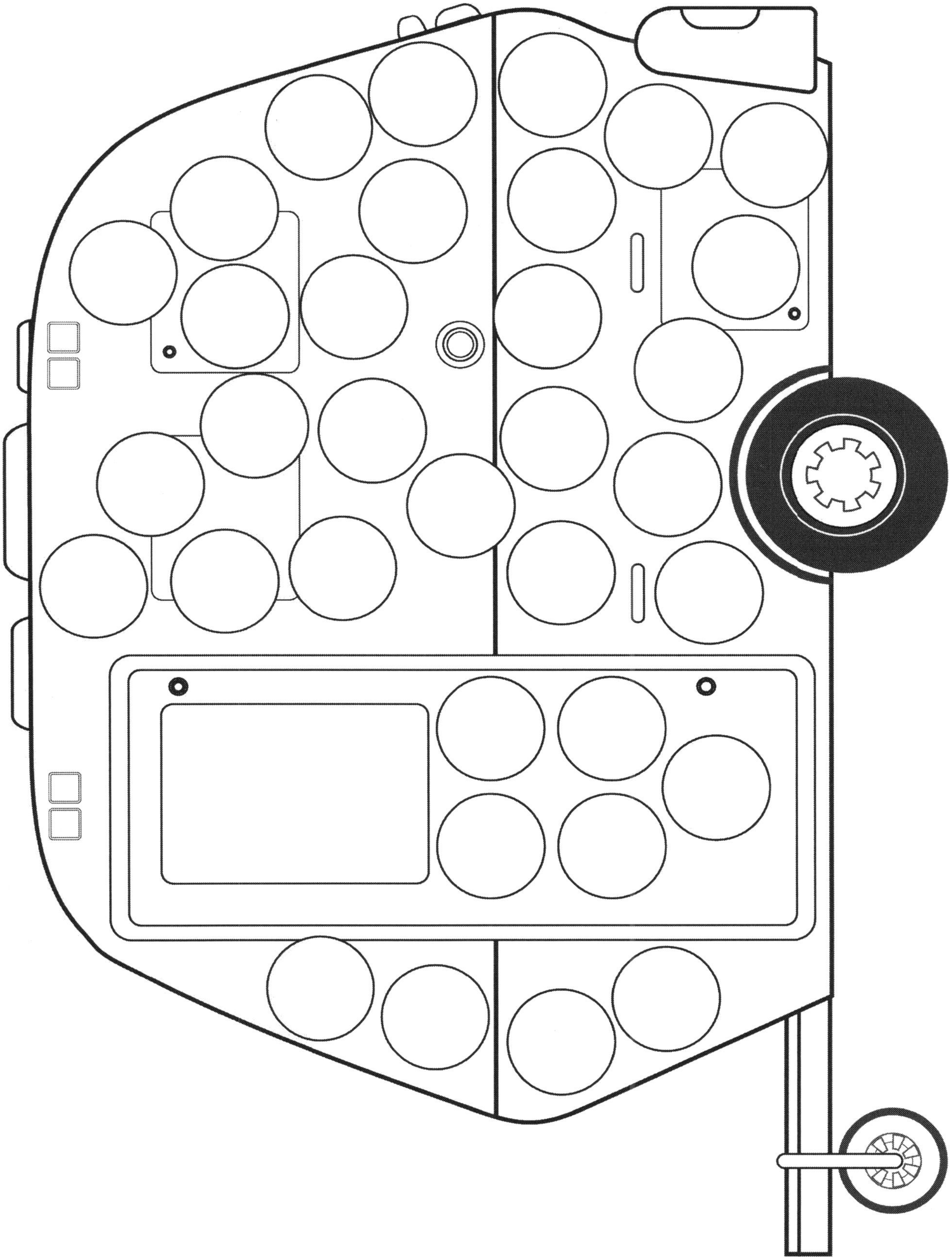

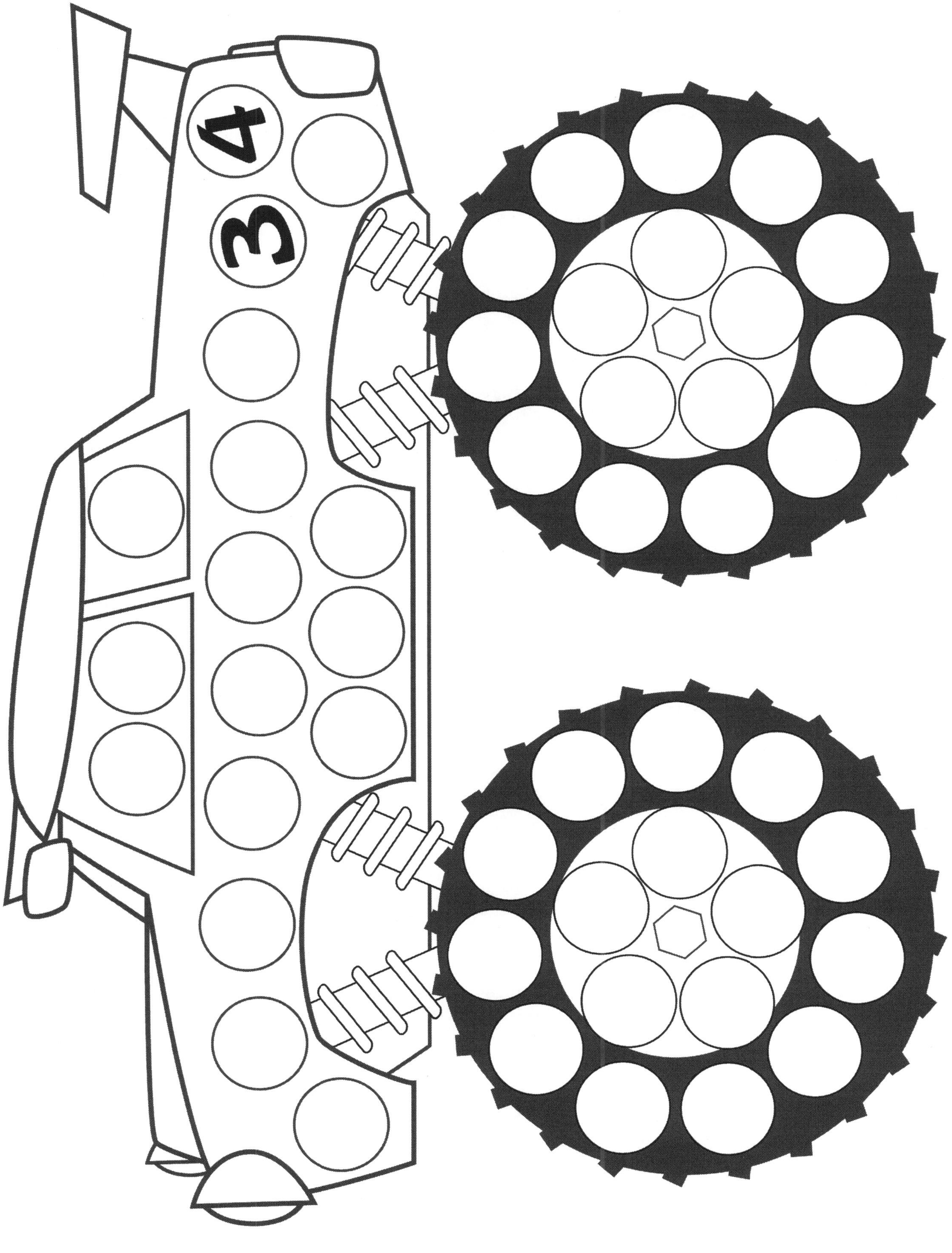
3
4

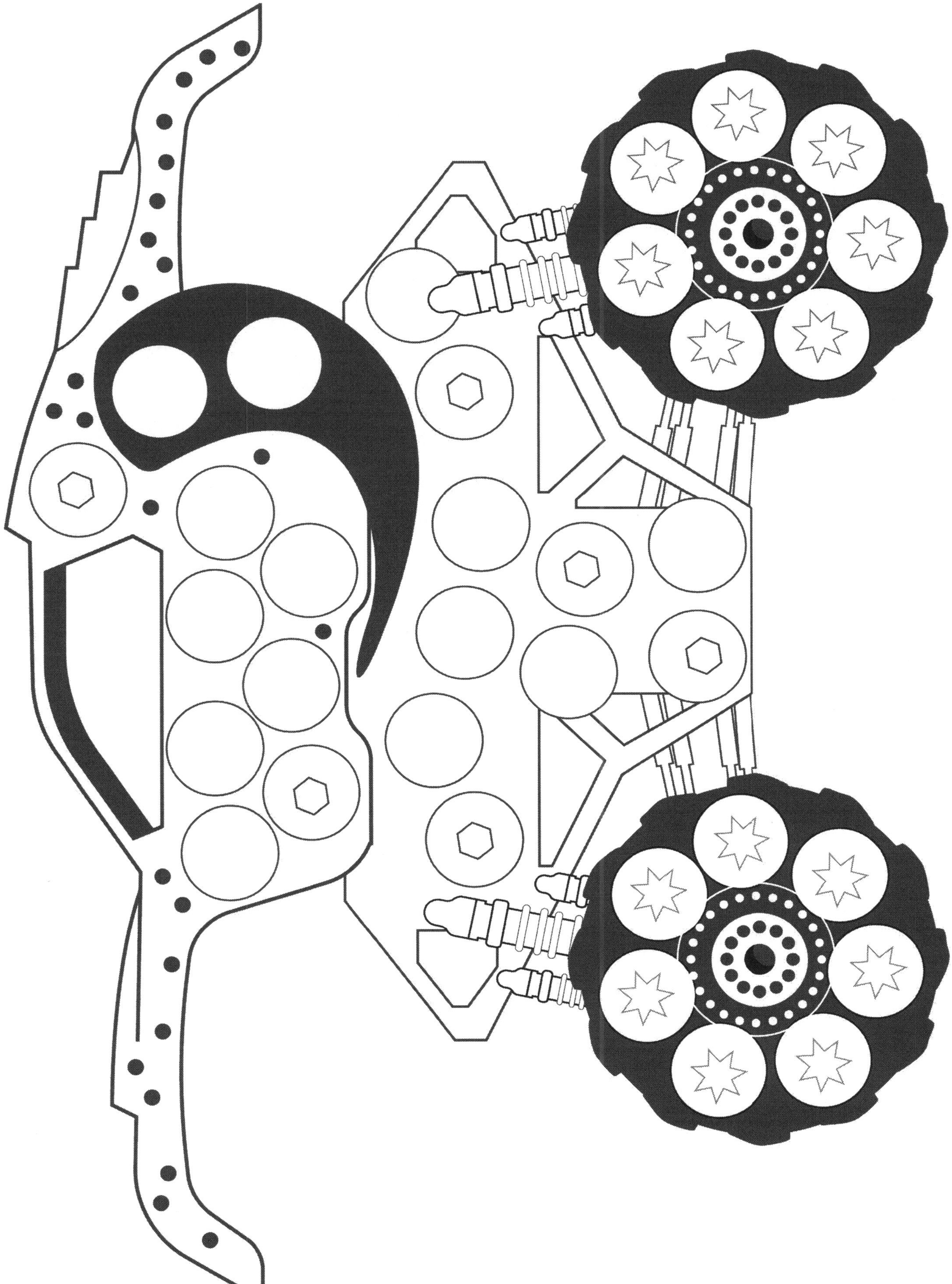

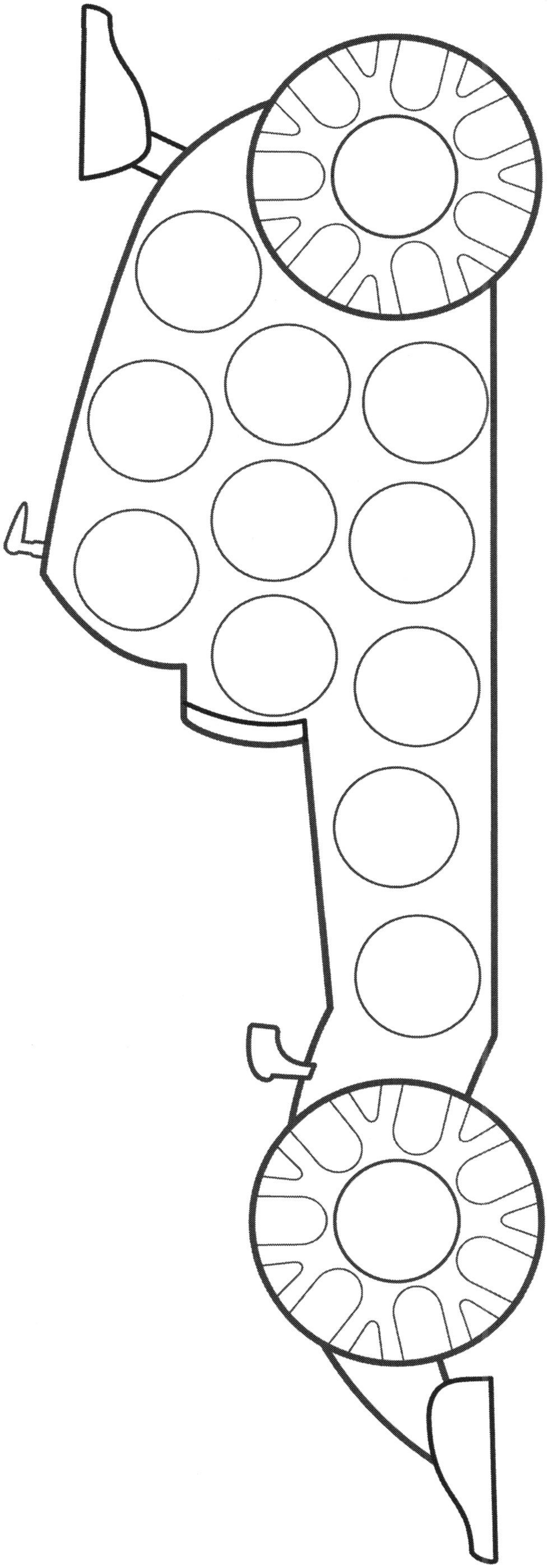

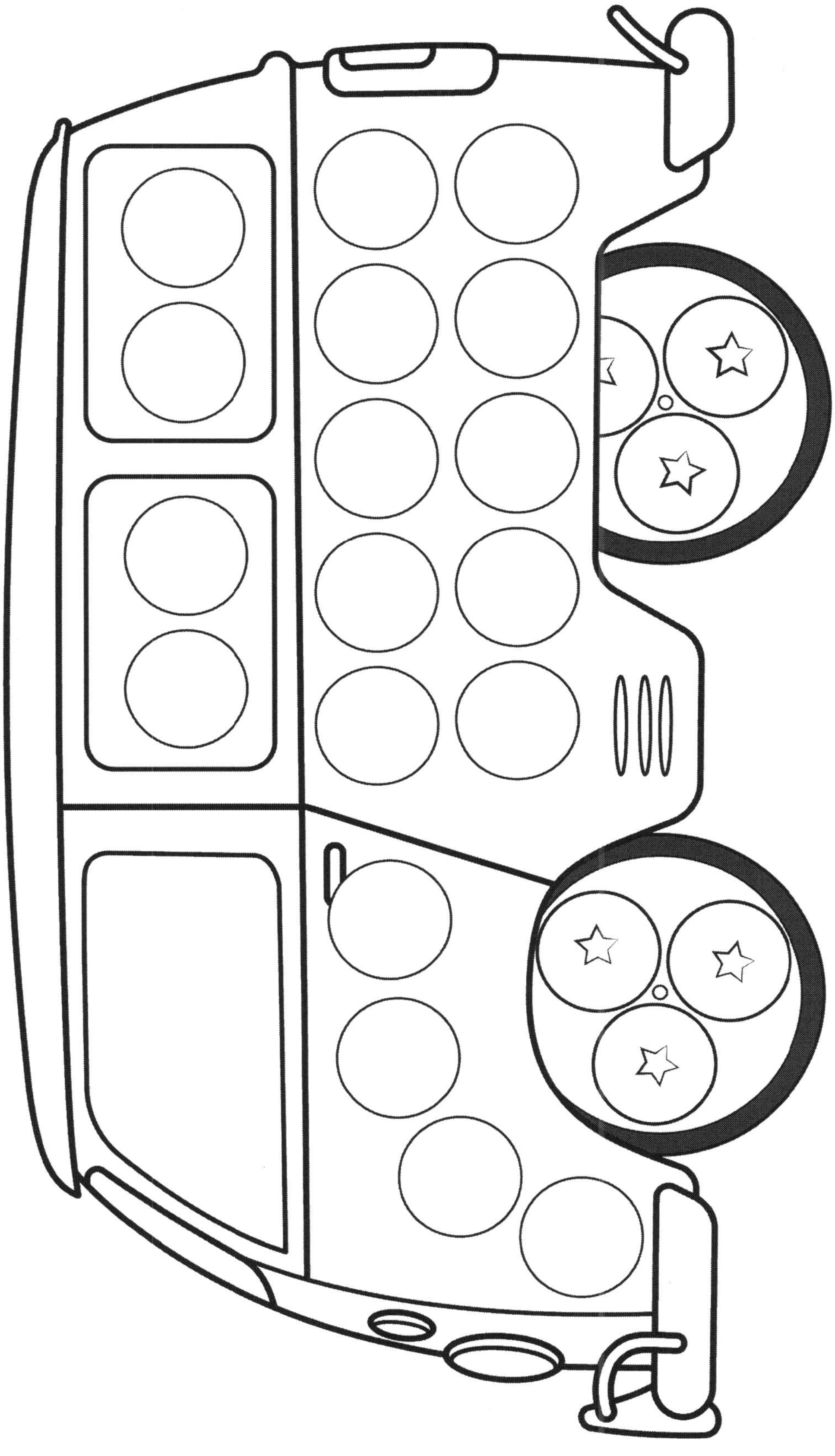

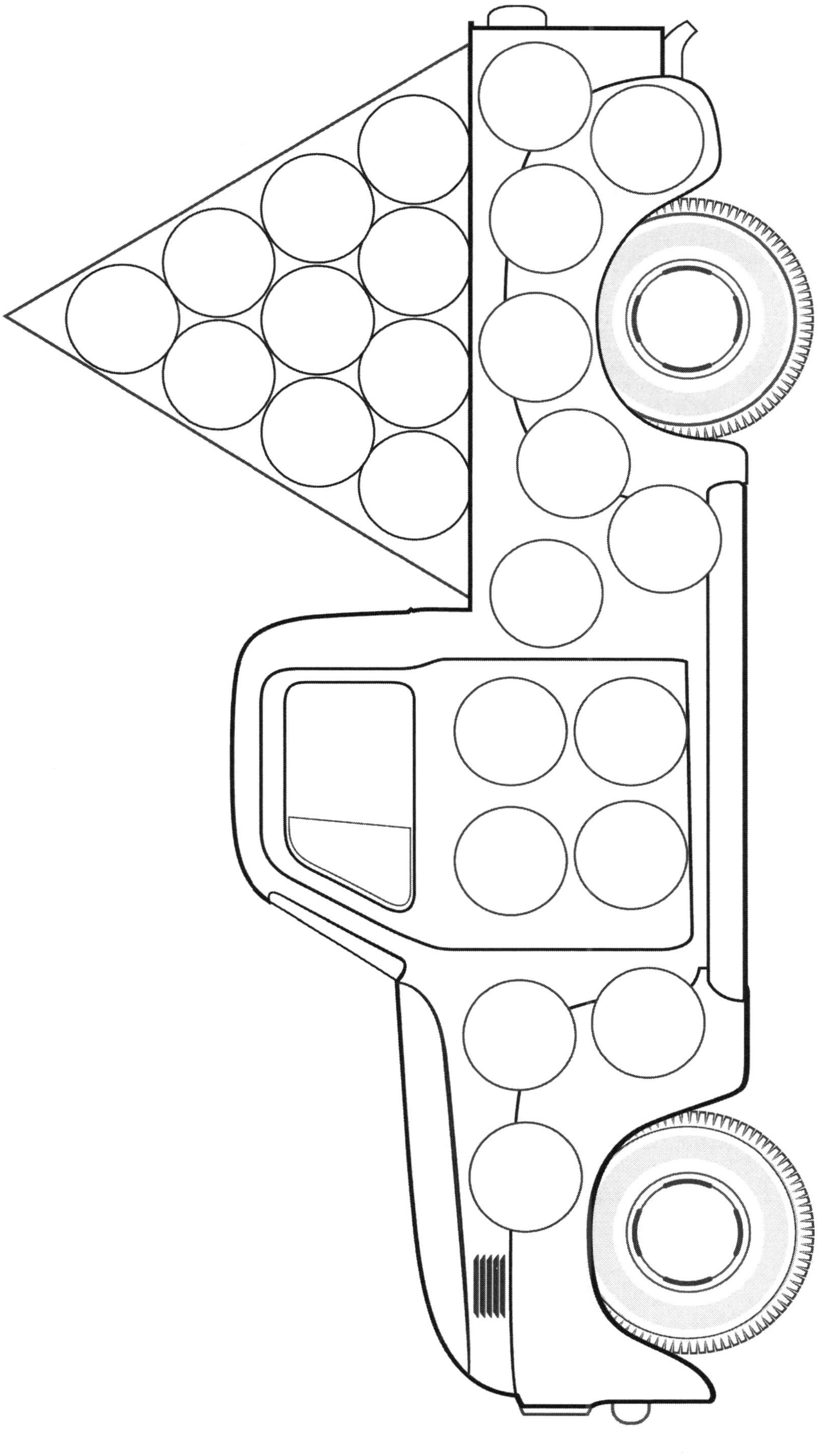

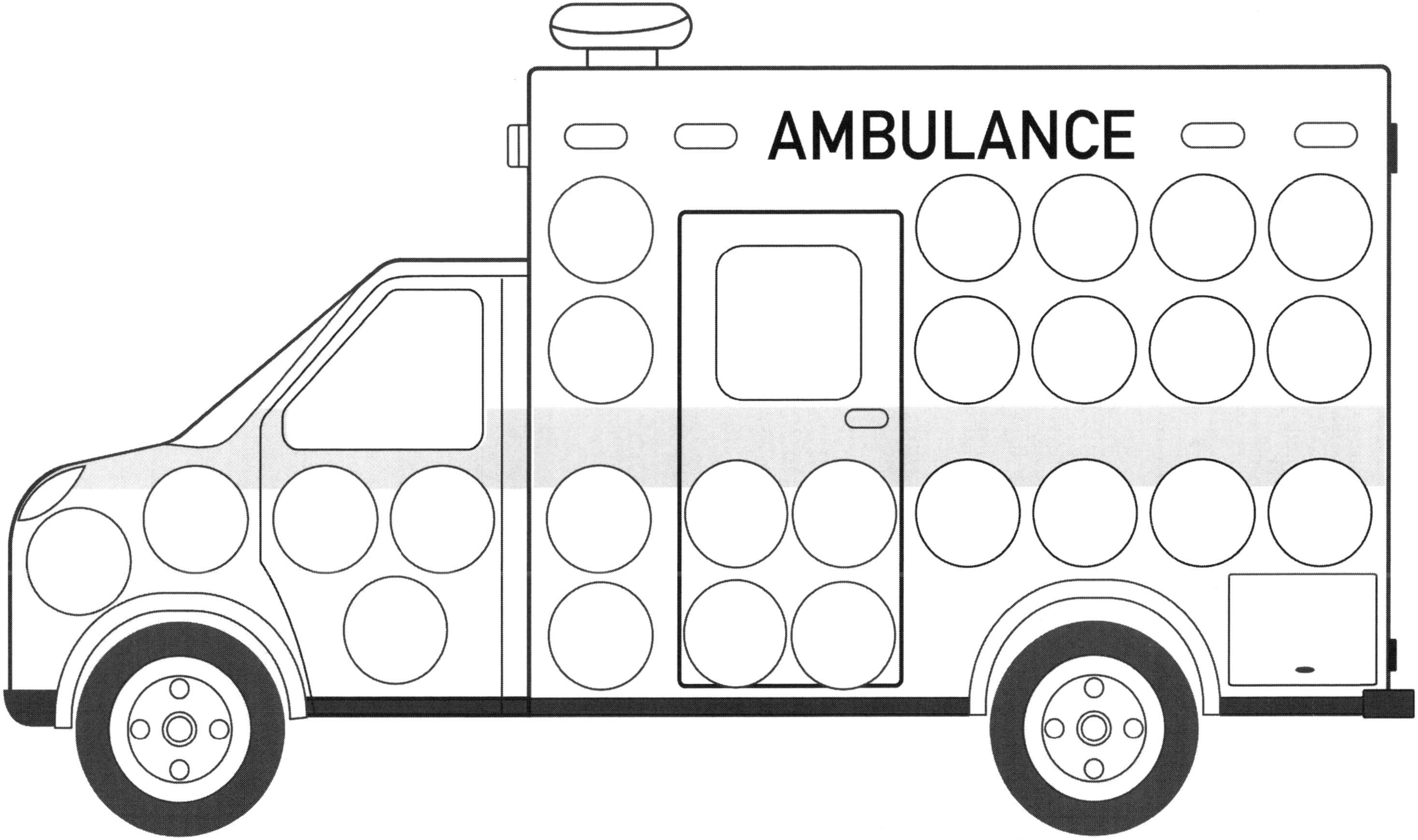
AMBULANCE

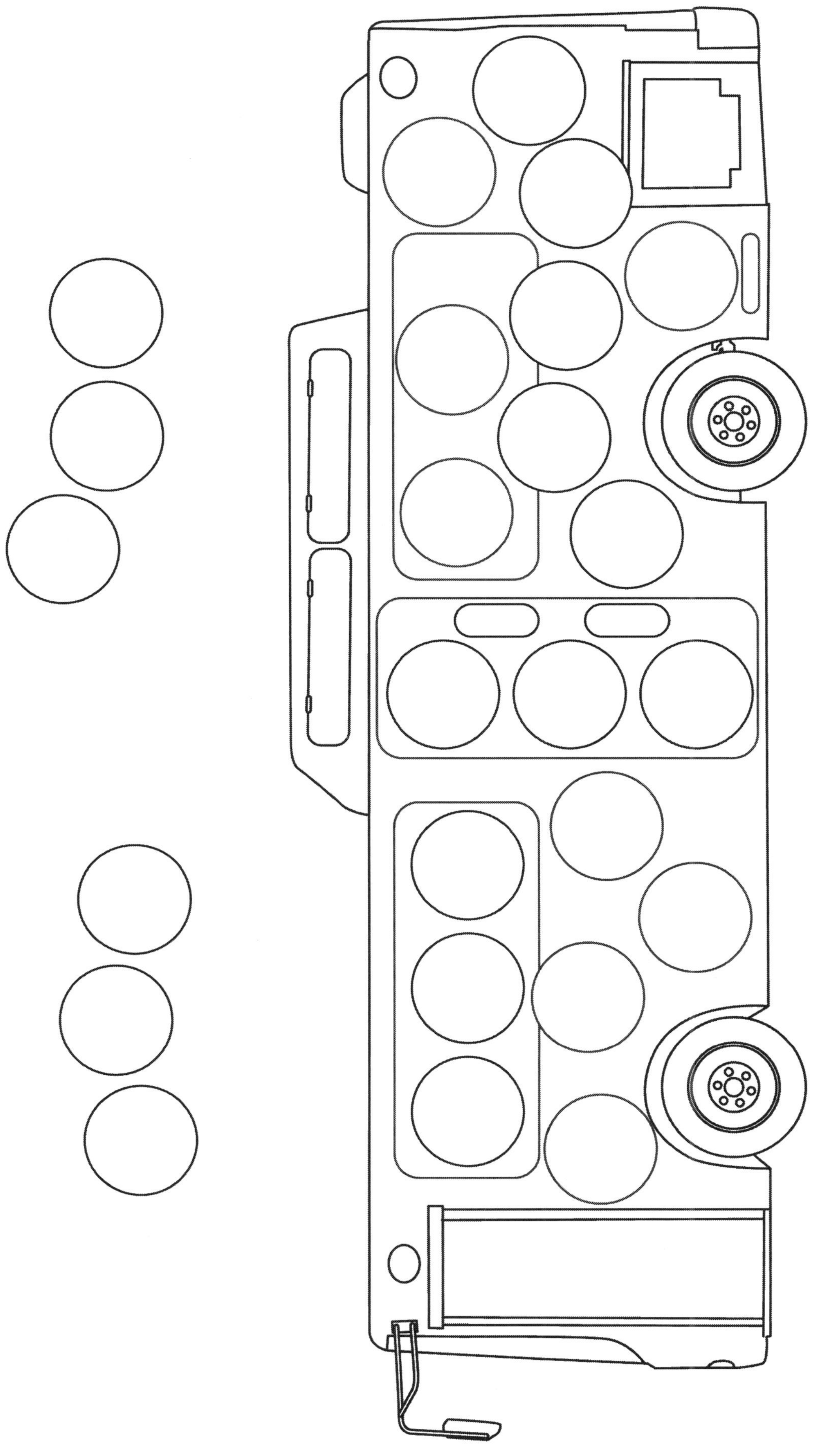

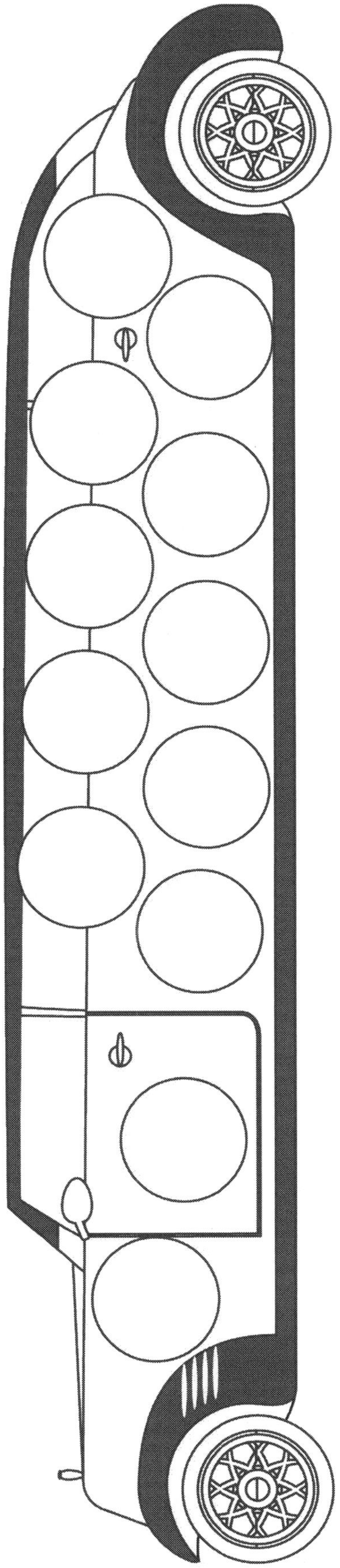

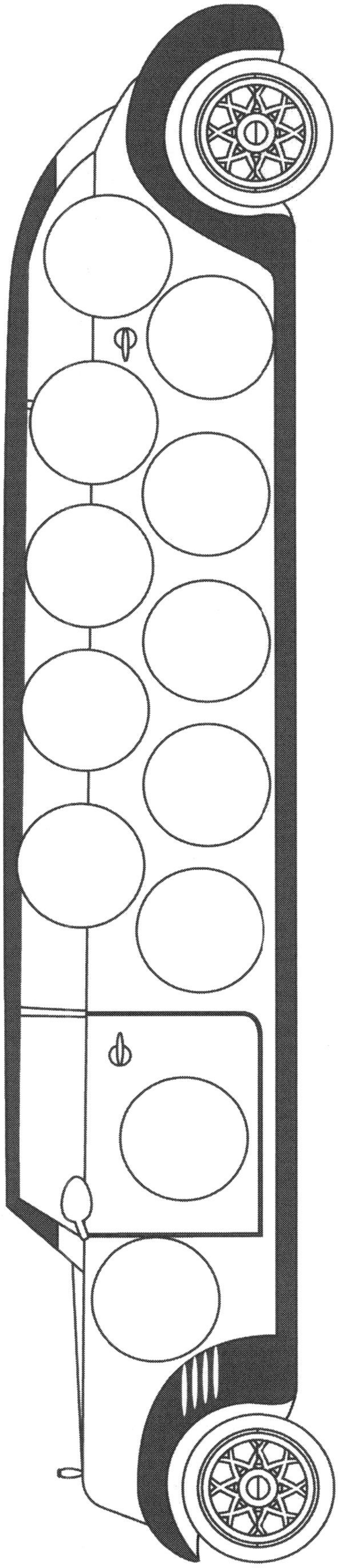

POLICE

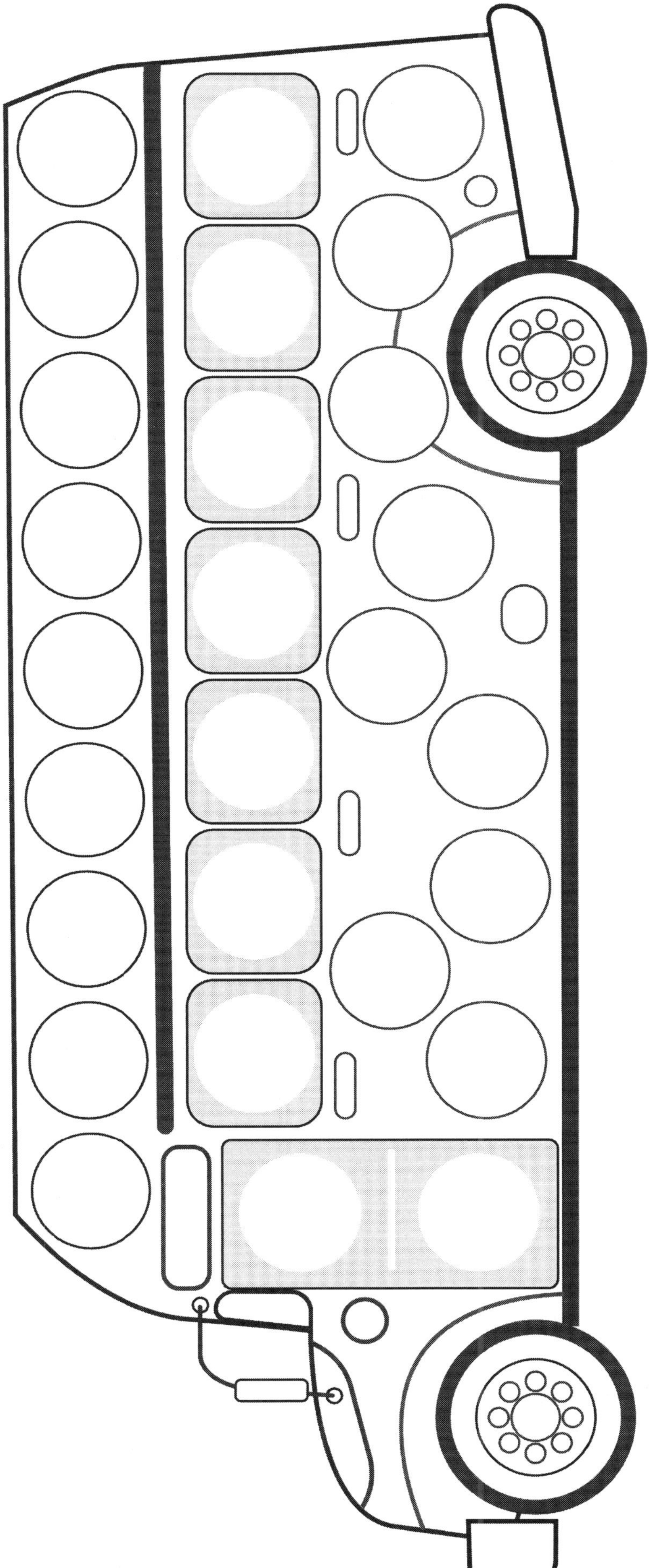

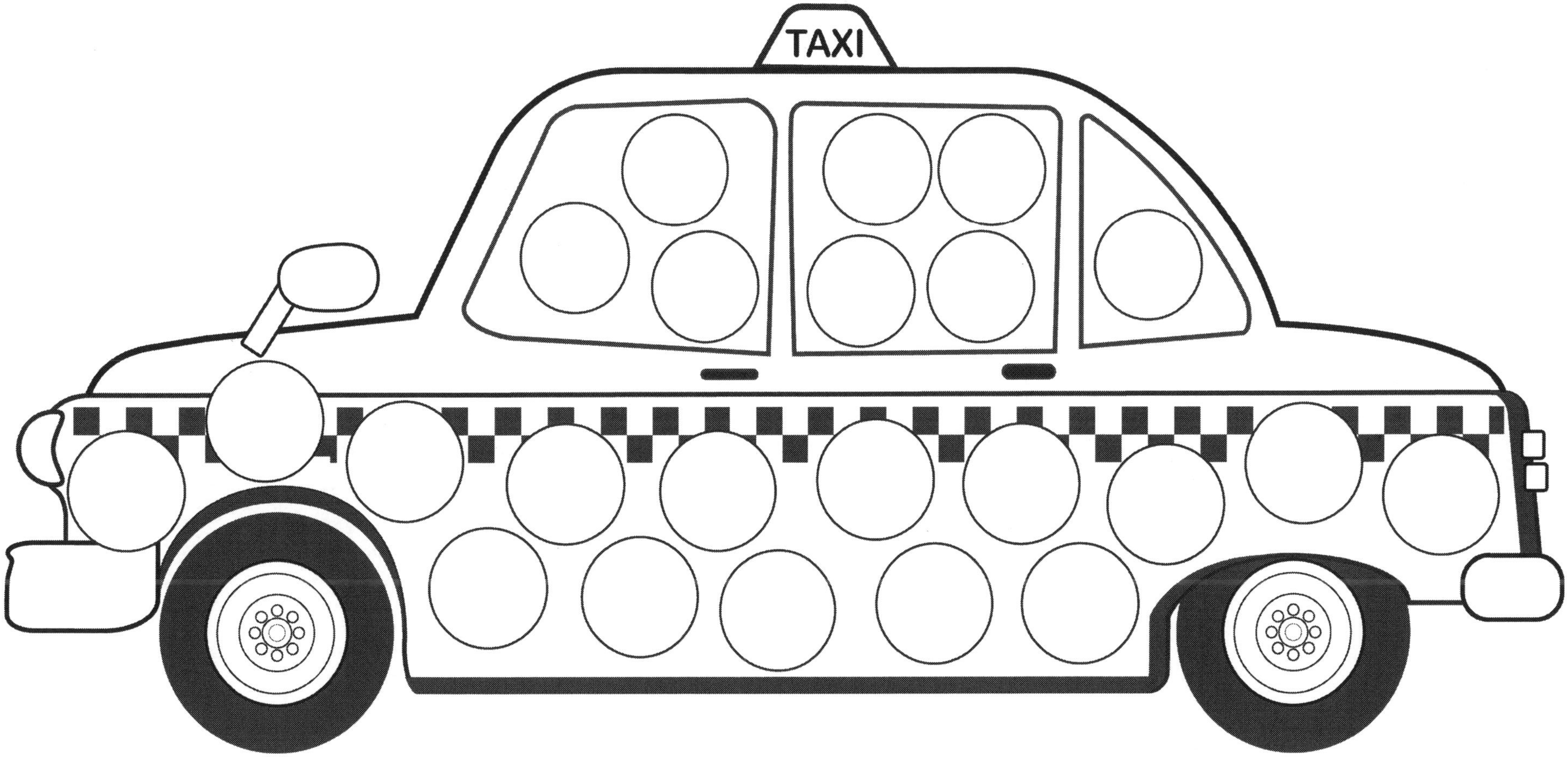
TAXI

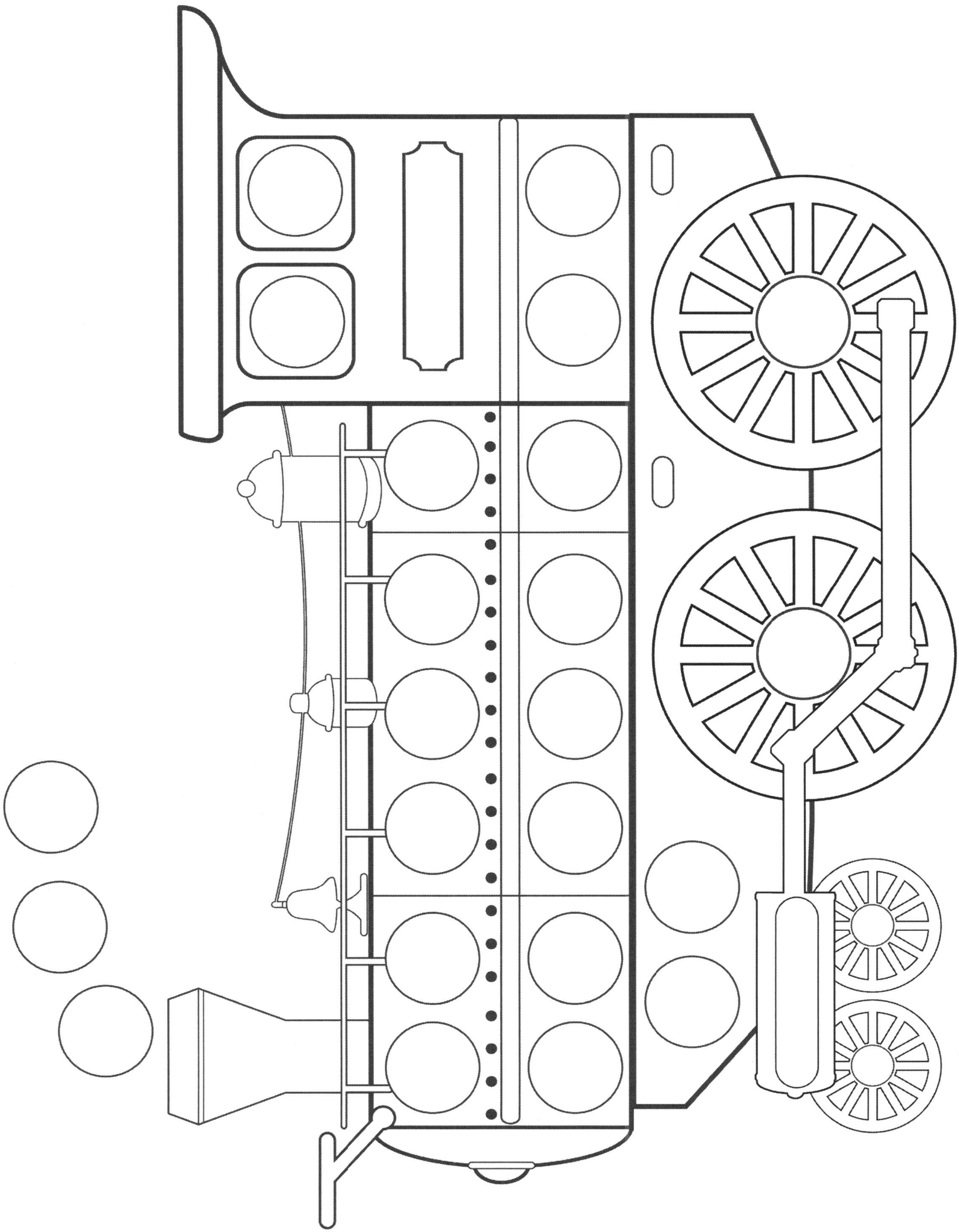

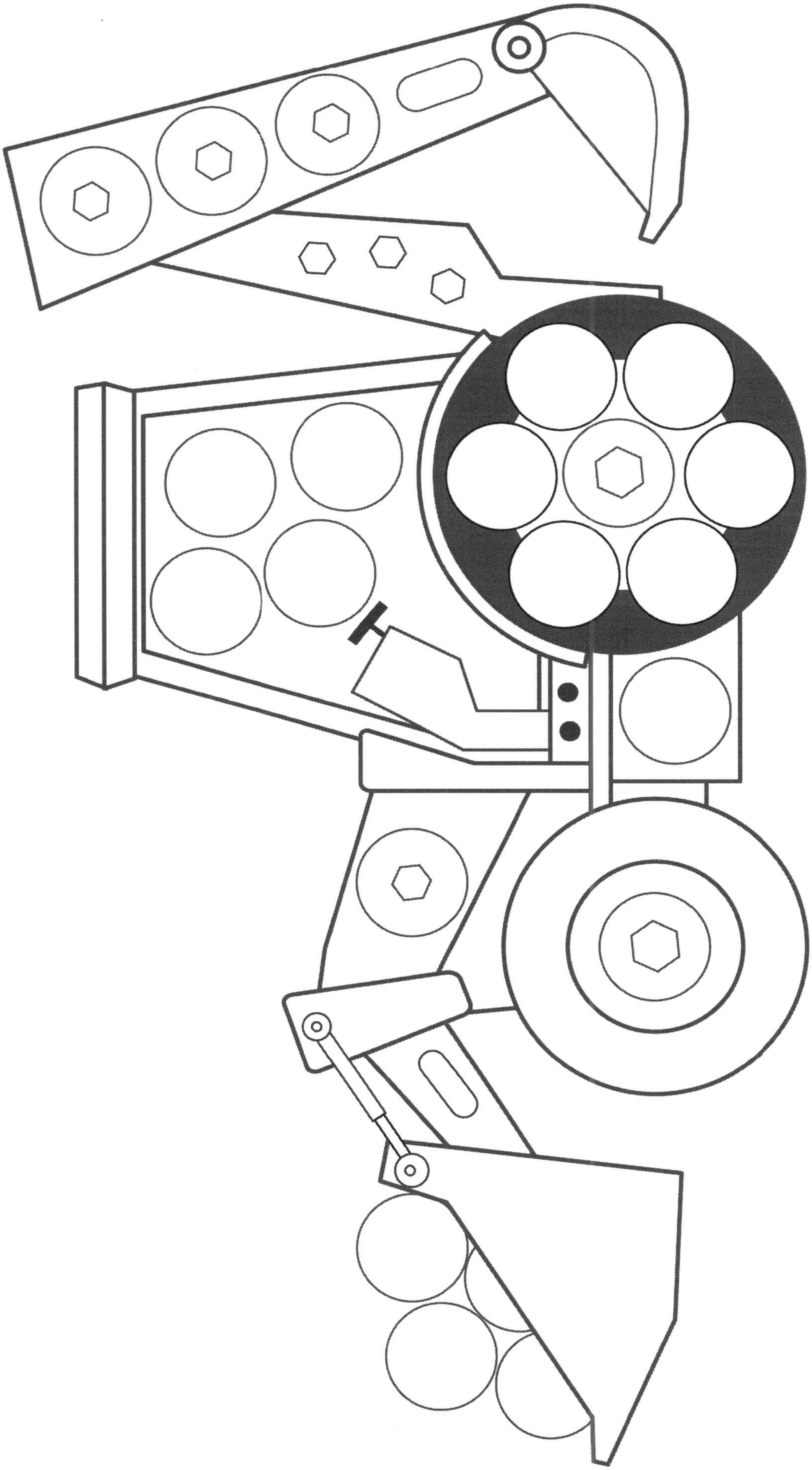

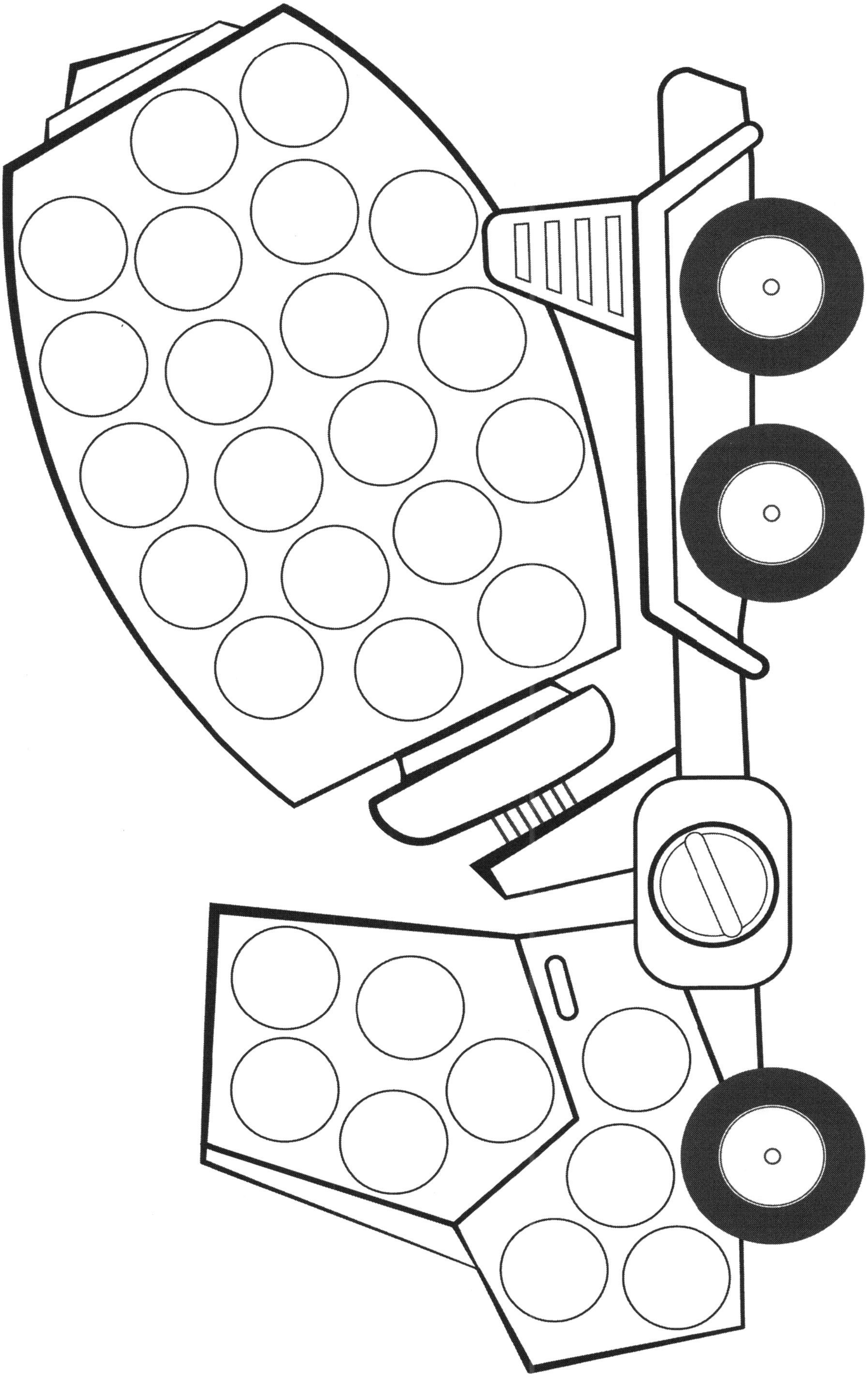

DINOSAUR PARADE

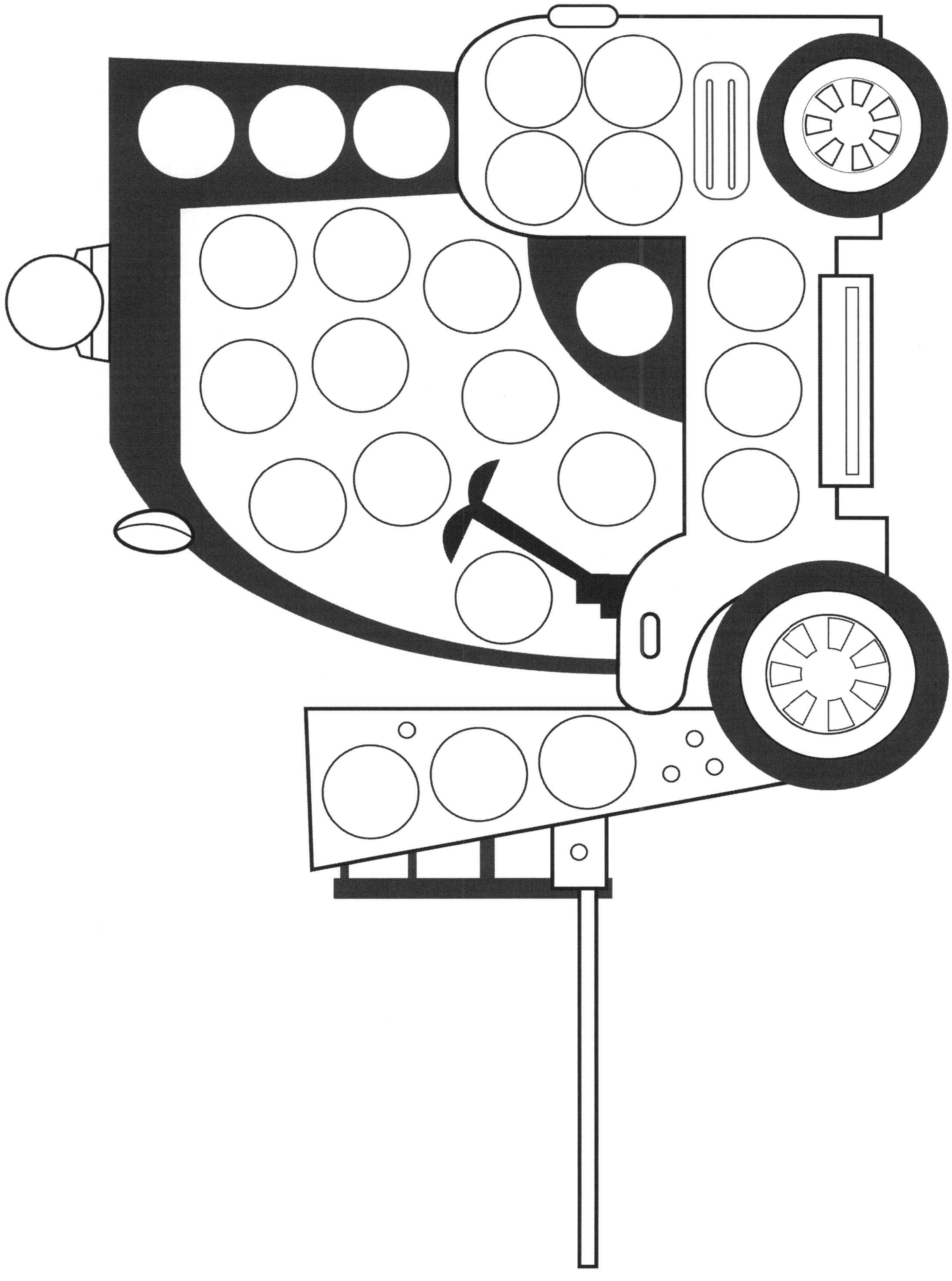

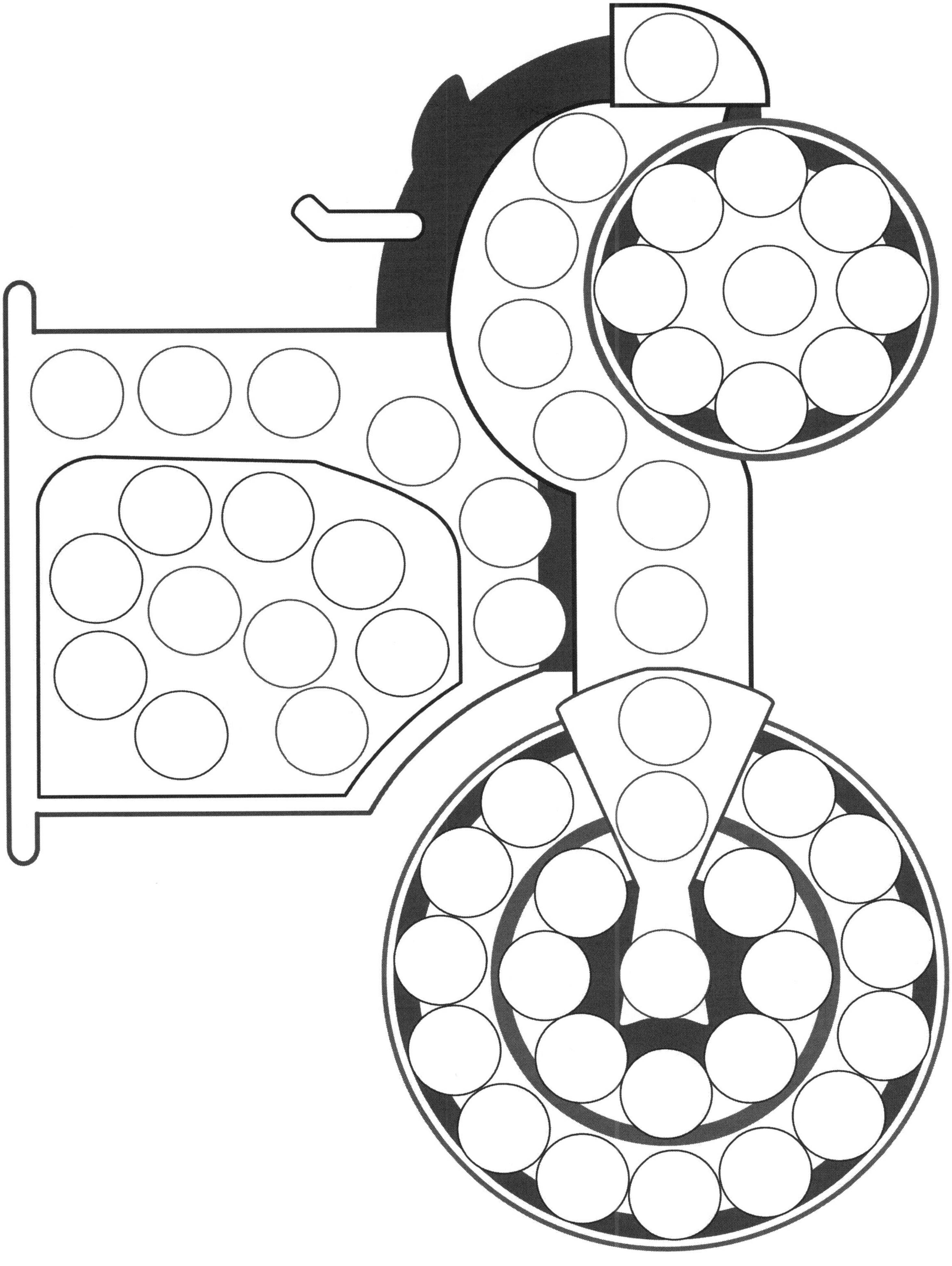

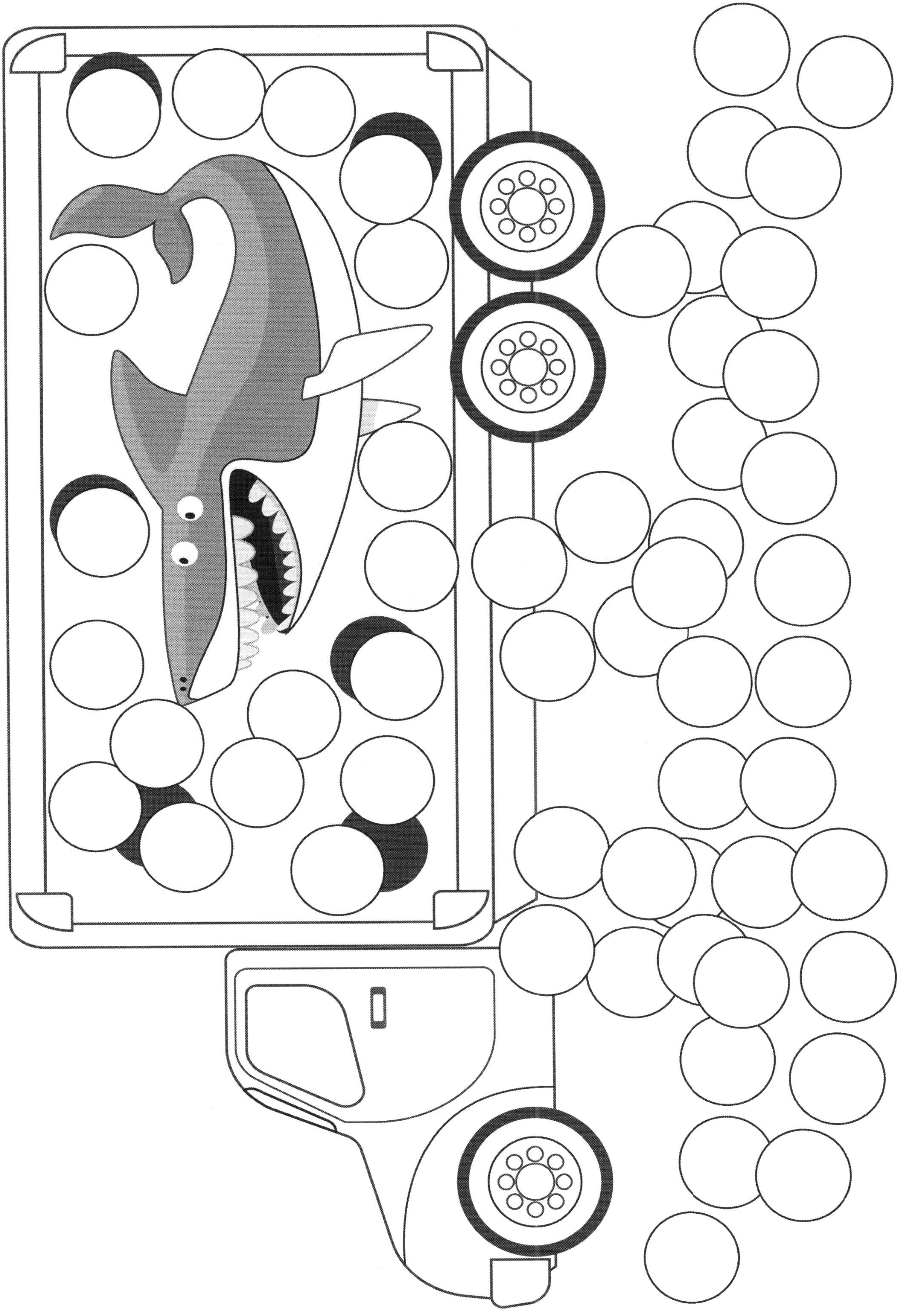

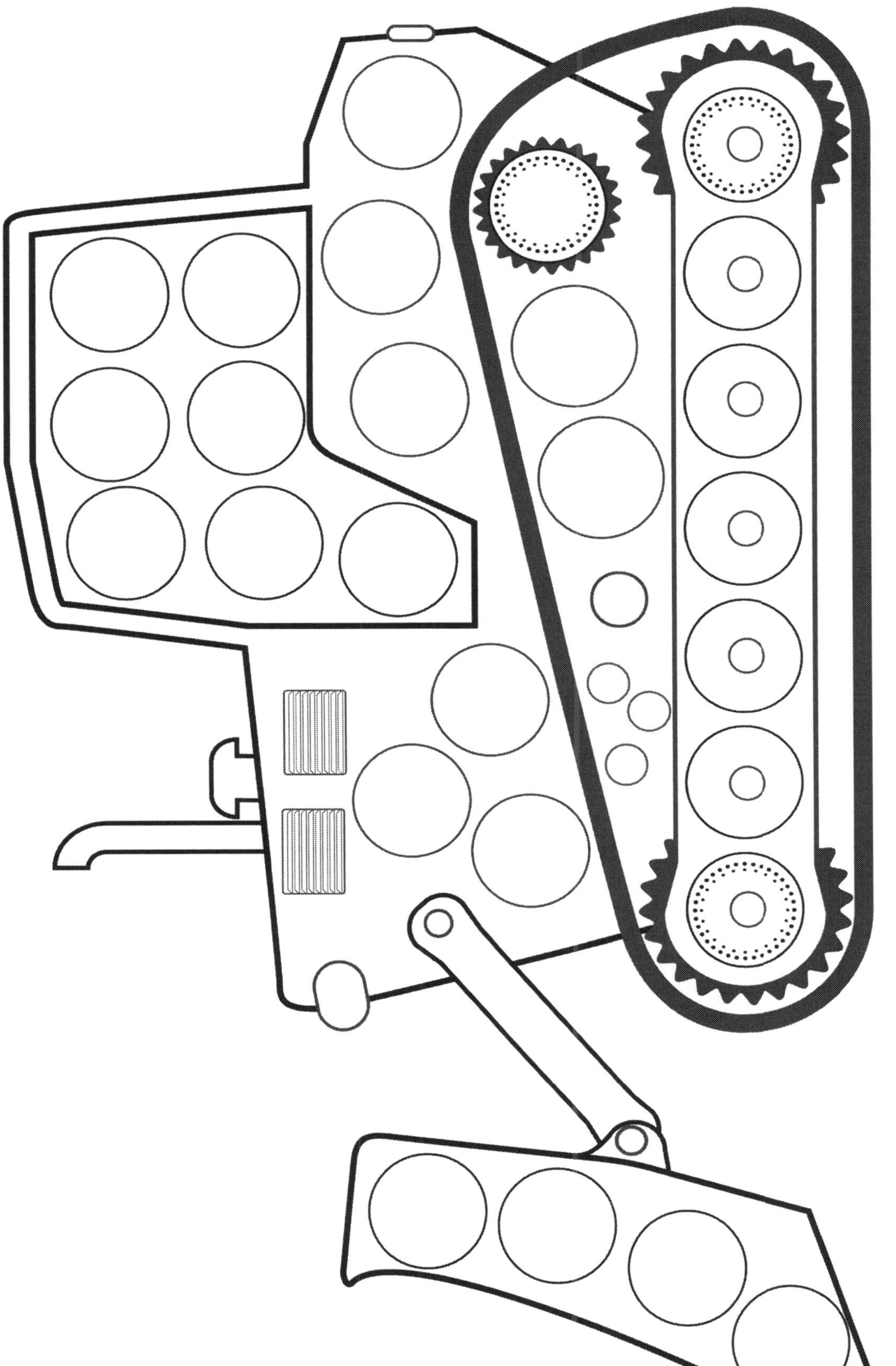

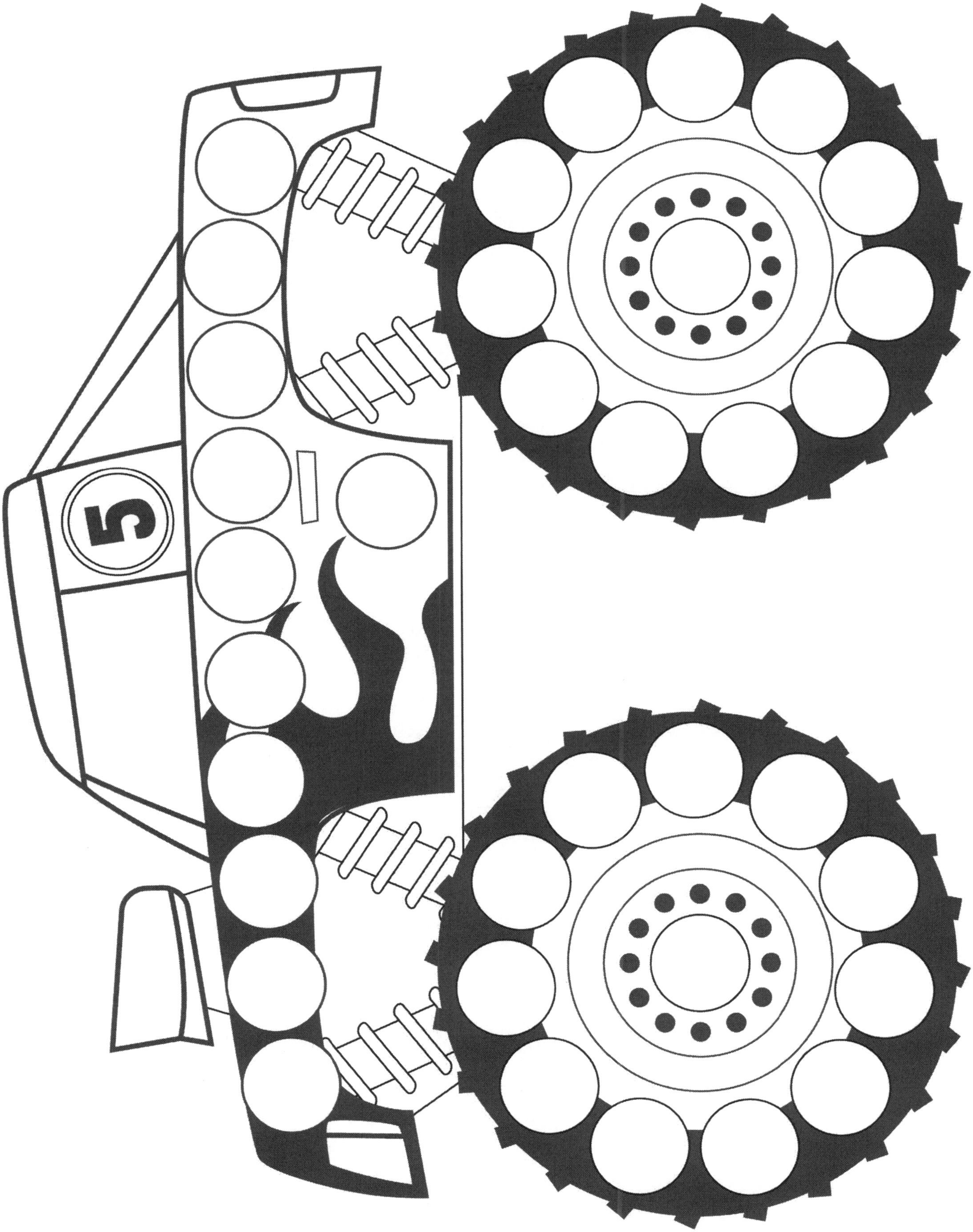

Bonus

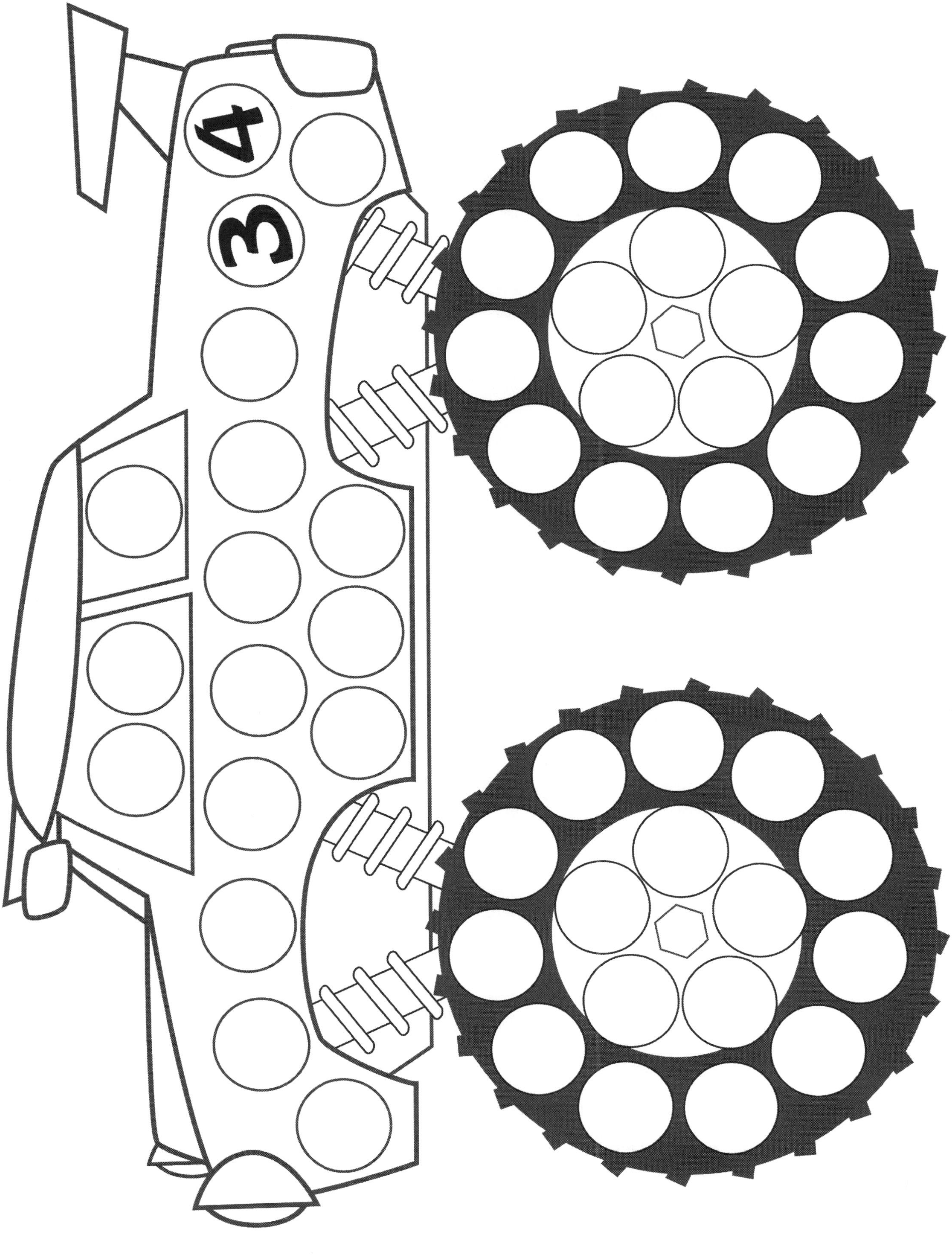
34

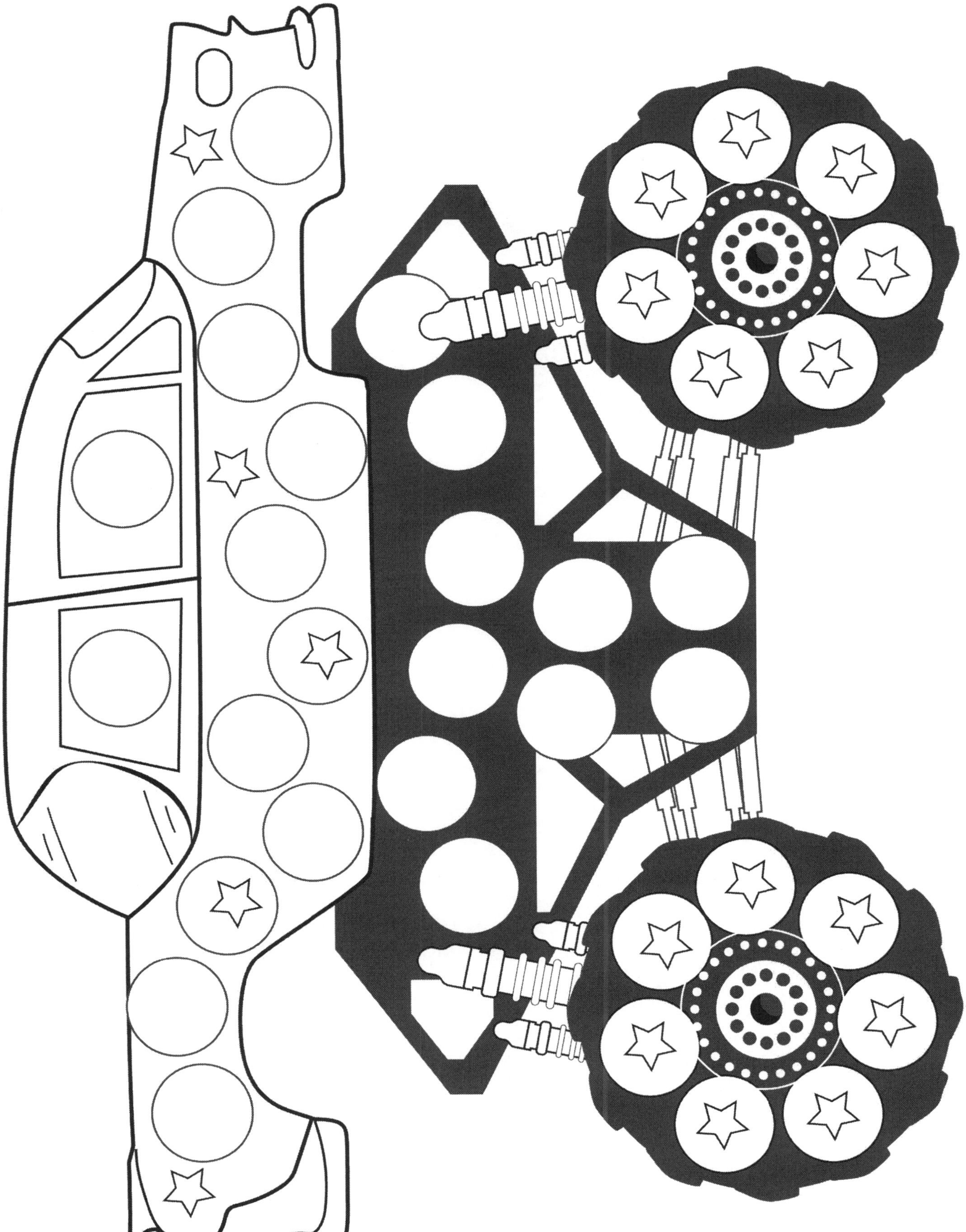

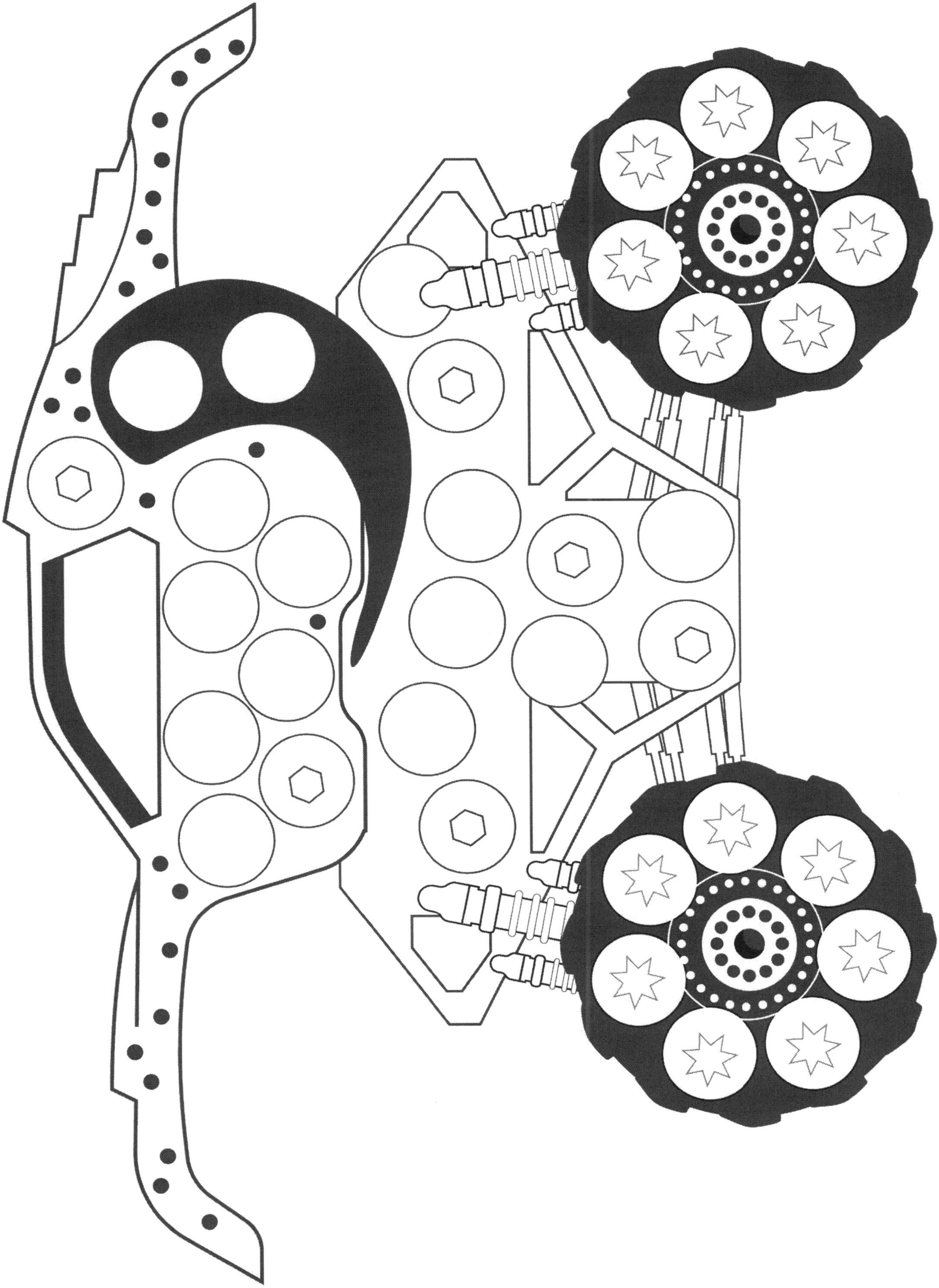

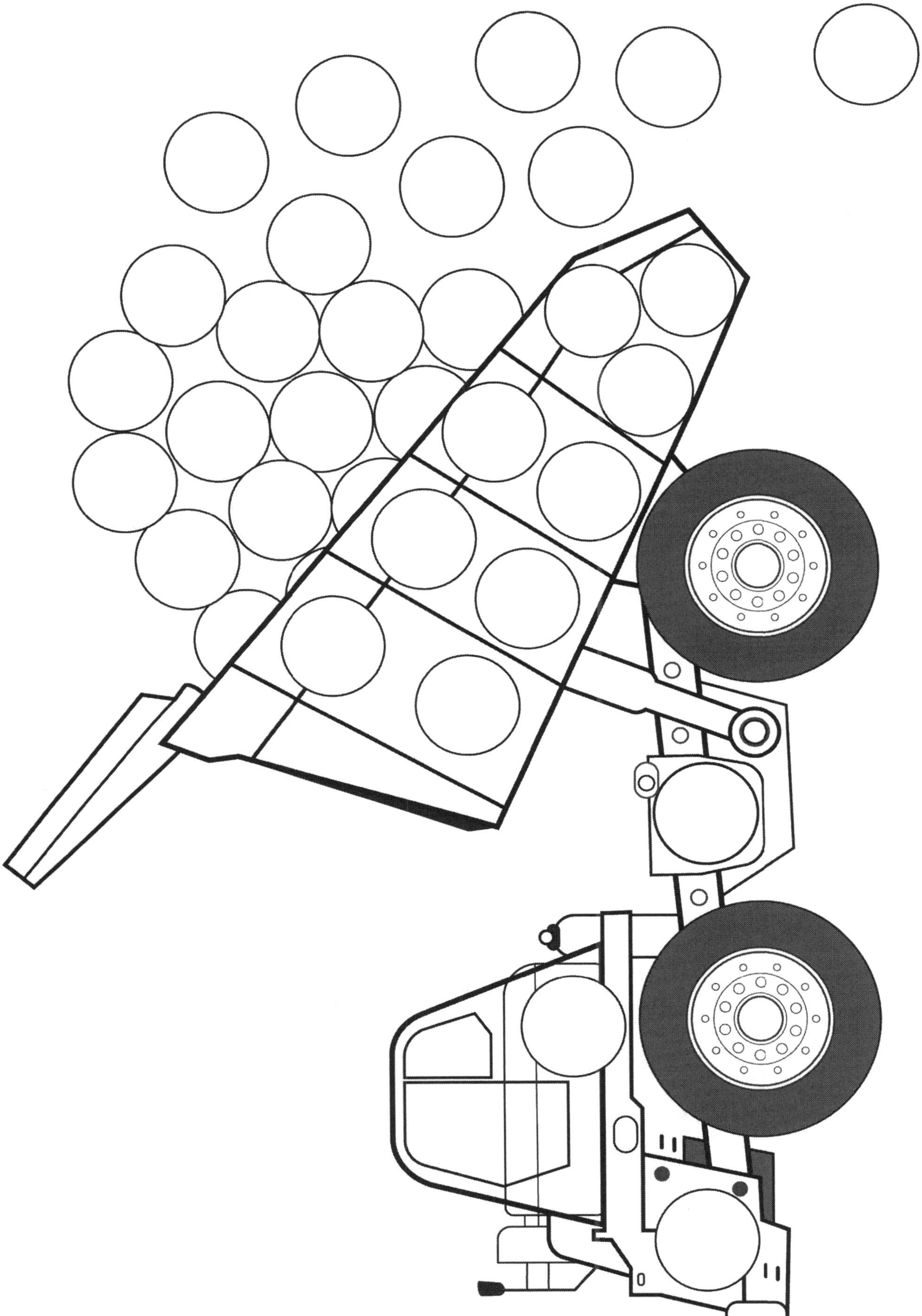

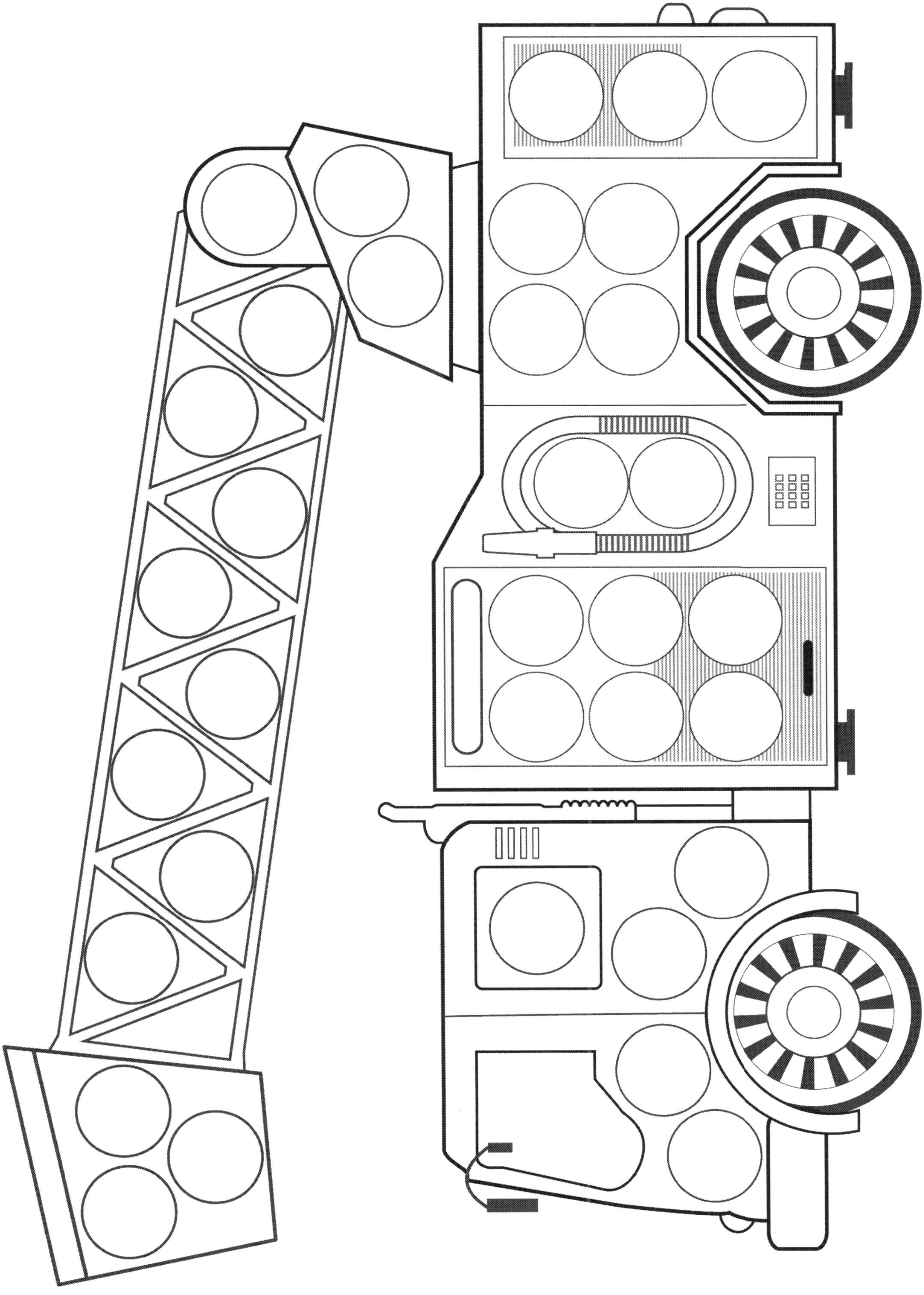

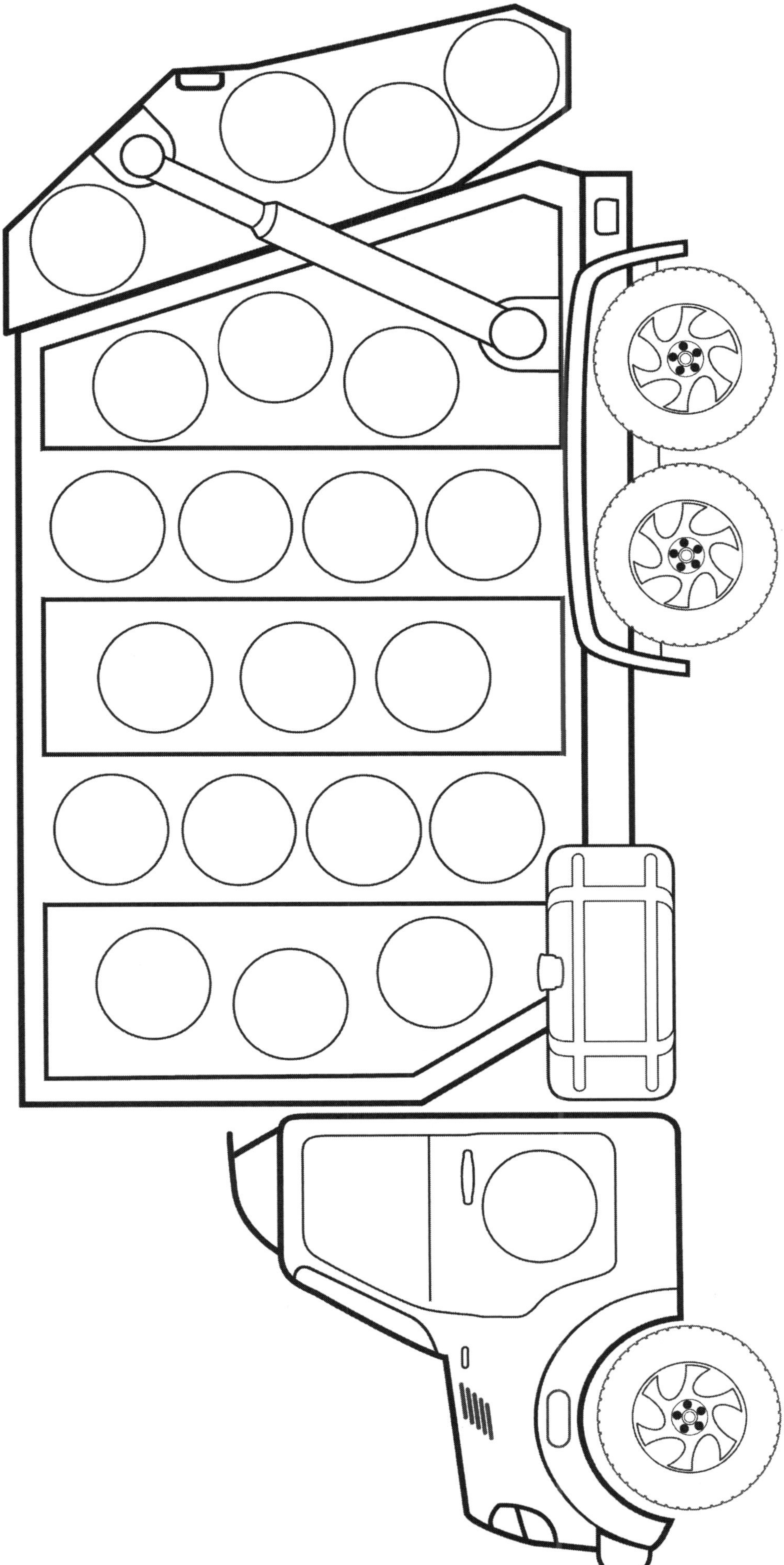

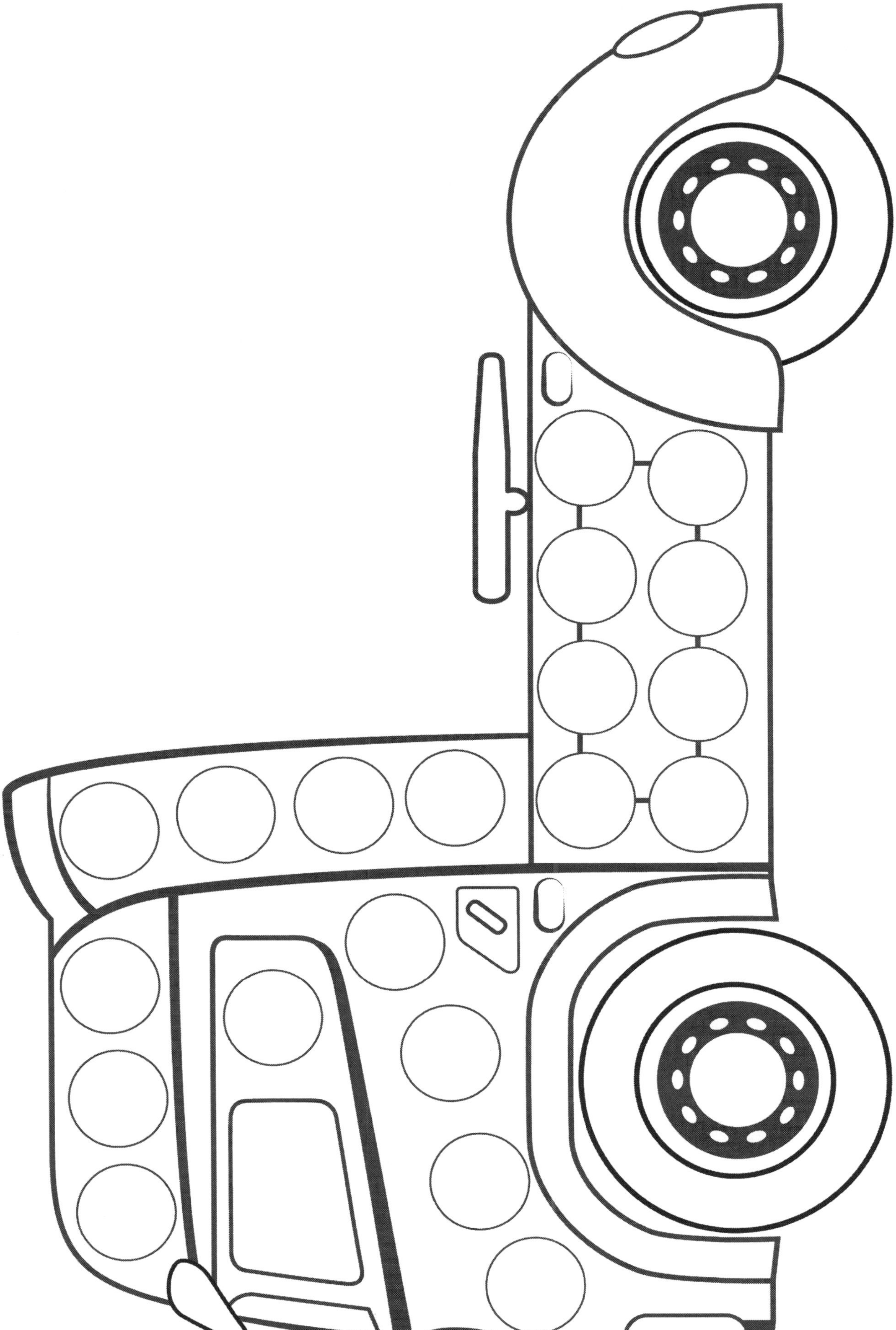

POLICE

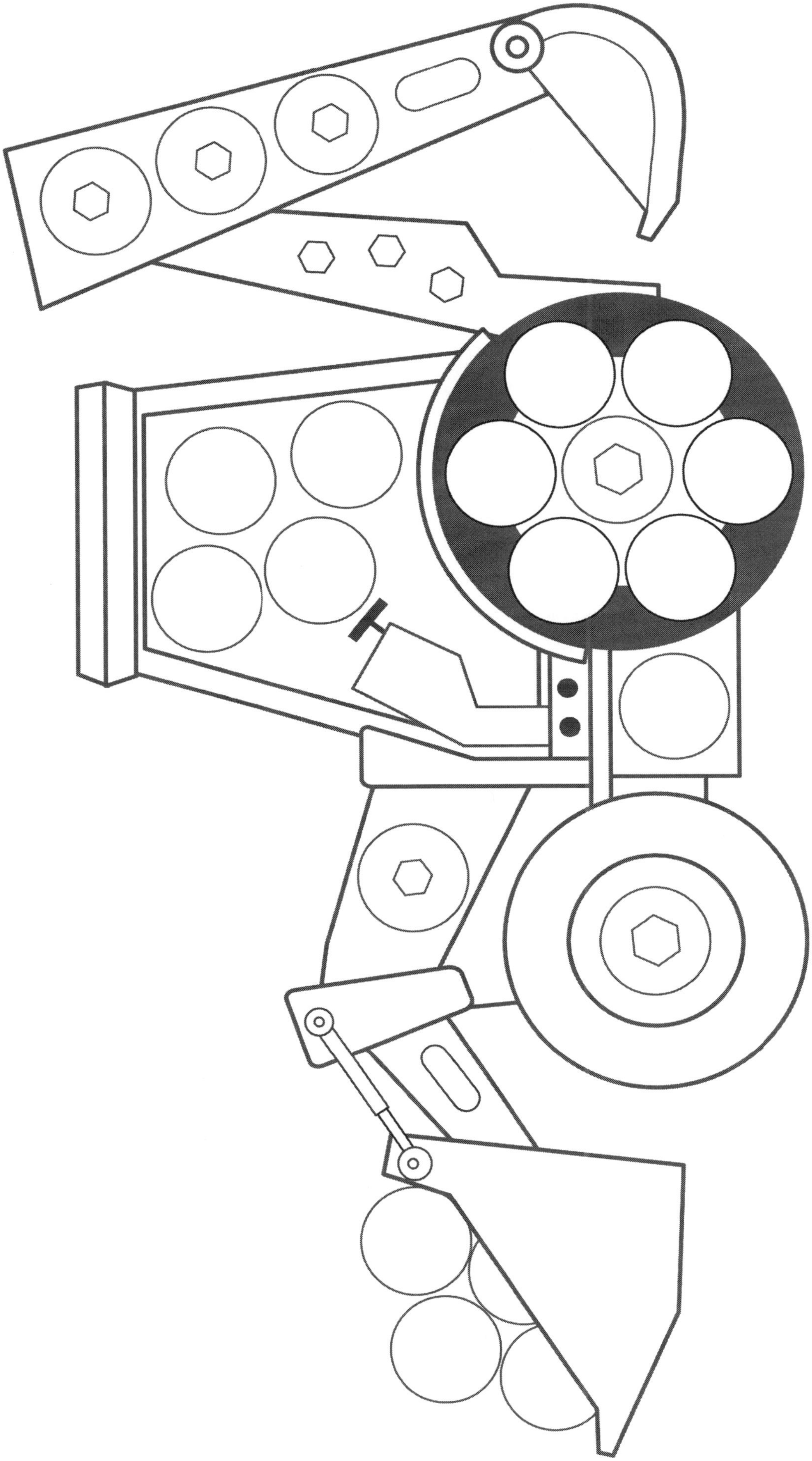

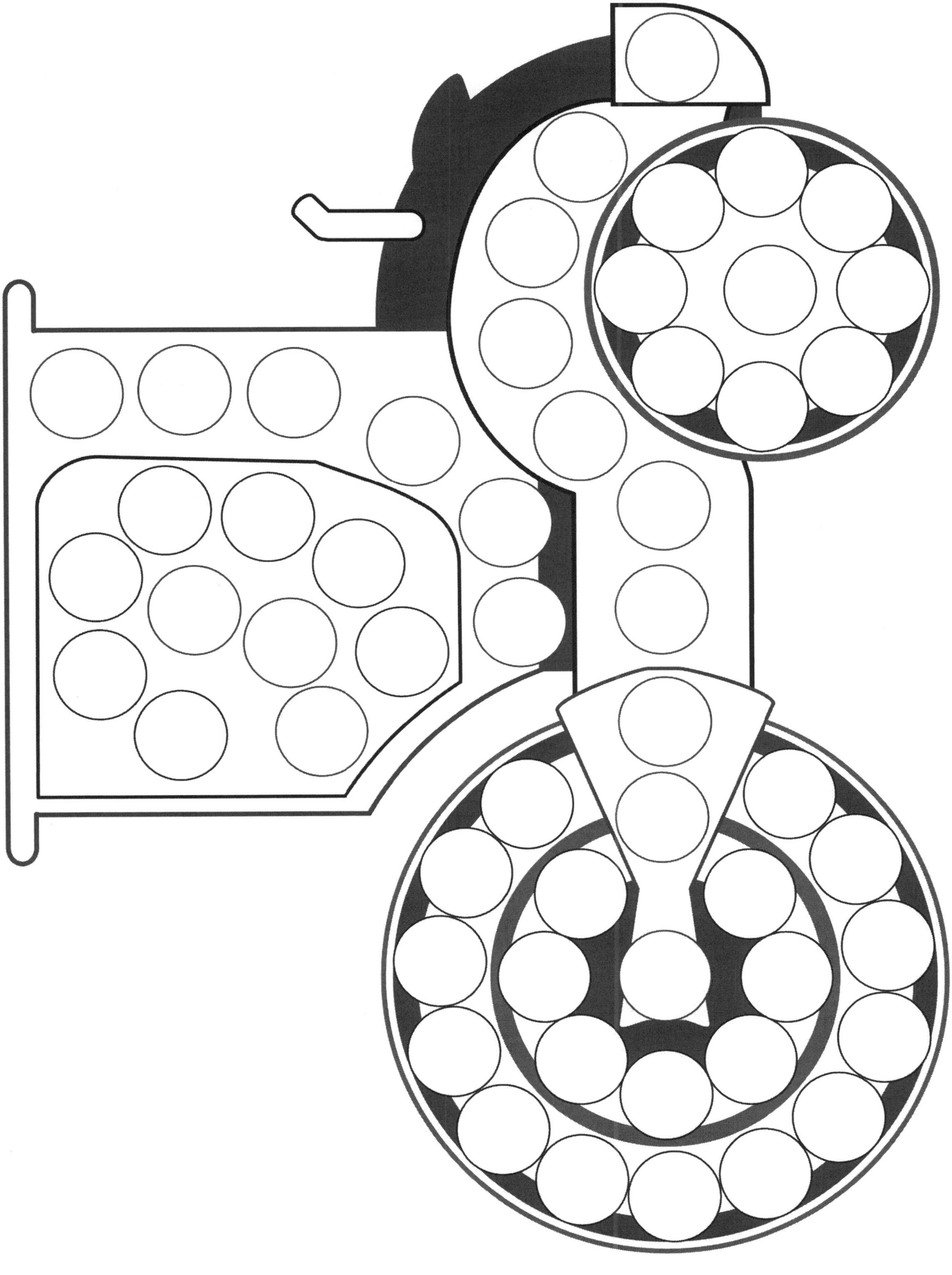

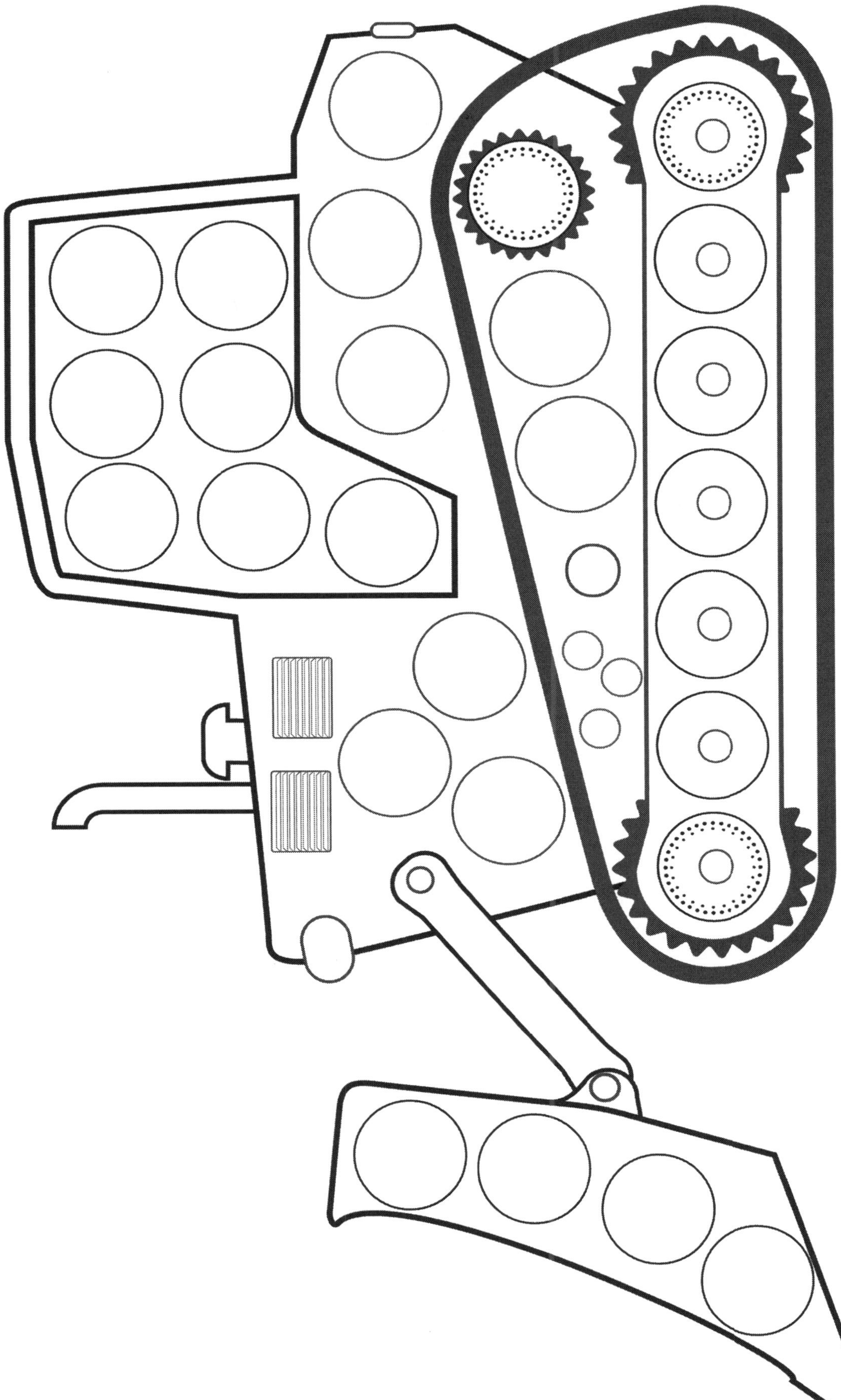

Blank Dot Markers

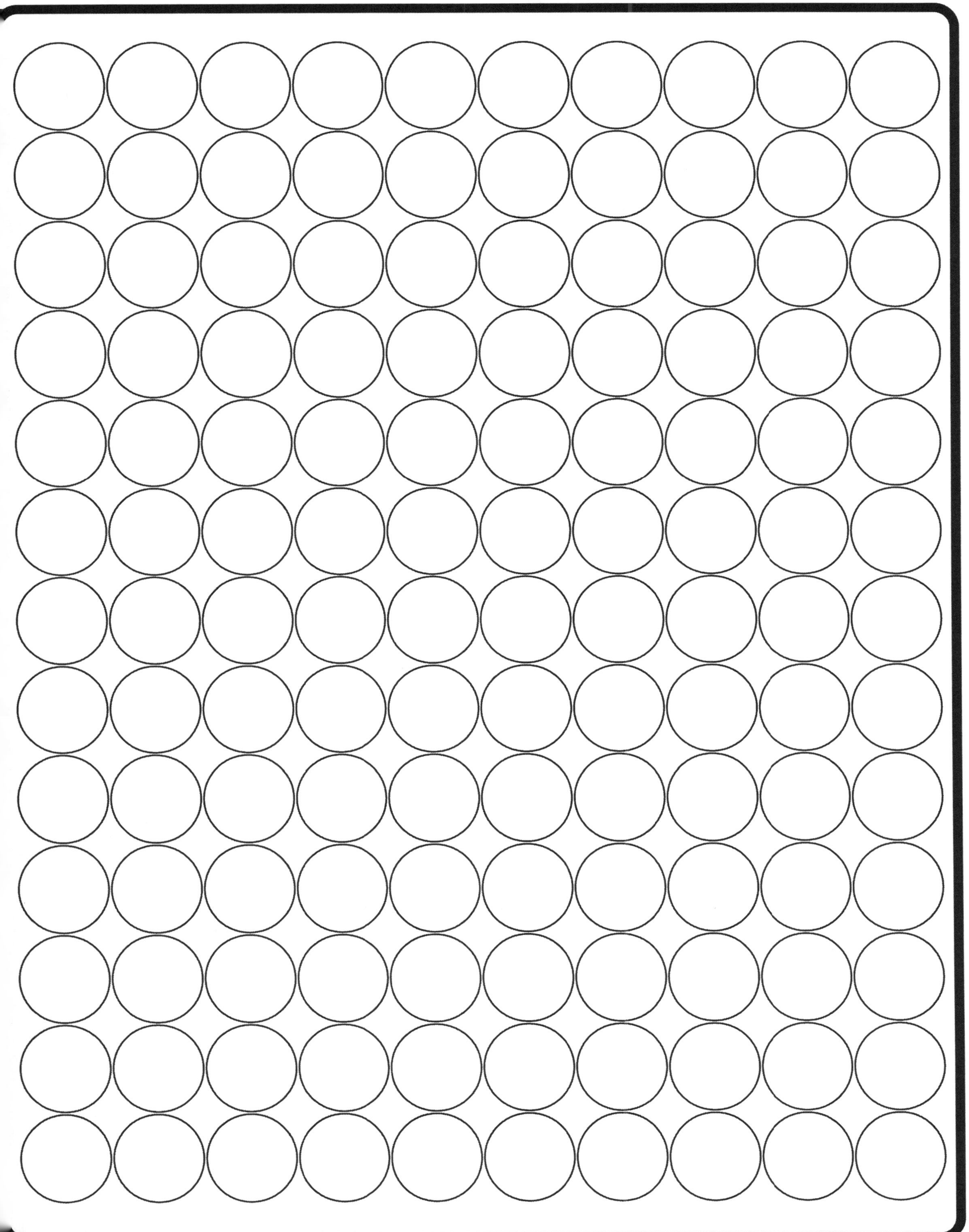

Made in the USA
Middletown, DE
15 October 2020

22016707R00062